FOUNDATIONS OF MODERN PSYCHOLOGY SERIES

Richard S. Lazarus, *Editor*

THE PSYCHOLOGICAL DEVELOPMENT OF THE CHILD, Paul H. Mussen

TESTS AND MEASUREMENTS, Leona E. Tyler

MOTIVATION AND EMOTION, Edward J. Murray

PERSONALITY AND ADJUSTMENT, Richard S. Lazarus

CLINICAL PSYCHOLOGY, Julian B. Rotter

SENSORY PSYCHOLOGY, Conrad G. Mueller

PERCEPTION, Julian E. Hochberg

LEARNING, Sarnoff A. Mednick

LANGUAGE AND THOUGHT, John B. Carroll

SOCIAL PSYCHOLOGY, William W. Lambert and Wallace E. Lambert

PHYSIOLOGICAL PSYCHOLOGY, Philip Teitelbaum

EDUCATIONAL PSYCHOLOGY, Donald Ross Green

THE NATURE OF PSYCHOLOGICAL INQUIRY, Ray Hyman

ORGANIZATIONAL PSYCHOLOGY, Edgar H. Schein

DONALD ROSS GREEN

Associate Professor of Teacher Education and Psychology, Emory University; researcher and author of articles in the fields of learning, motivation, cognitive development, teacher education, and teaching methods.

Educational
Psychology

PRENTICE-HALL, INC., *Englewood Cliffs, New Jersey*

EDUCATIONAL PSYCHOLOGY, Donald Ross Green

PRENTICE-HALL FOUNDATIONS
OF MODERN PSYCHOLOGY SERIES
Richard S. Lazarus, *Editor*

PRENTICE-HALL INTERNATIONAL, INC., *London*
PRENTICE-HALL OF AUSTRALIA, PTY., LTD., *Sydney*
PRENTICE-HALL OF CANADA, LTD., *Toronto*
PRENTICE-HALL OF INDIA PRIVATE LIMITED, *New Delhi*
PRENTICE-HALL OF JAPAN, INC., *Tokyo*
PRENTICE-HALL DE MEXICO, S.A., *Mexico City*

Designed by Harry Rinehart

C-24057(p), C-24058(c)

Foundations
of Modern Psychology
Series

The tremendous growth and vitality of psychology and its increasing fusion with the social and biological sciences demand a new approach to teaching at the introductory level. The basic course, geared as it usually is to a single text that tries to skim everything—that sacrifices depth for superficial breadth —is no longer adequate. Psychology has become too diverse for any one man, or a few men, to write about with complete authority. The alternative, a book that ignores many essential areas in order to present more comprehensively and effectively a particular aspect or view of psychology, is also insufficient. For in this solution, many key areas are simply not communicated to the student at all.

The Foundations of Modern Psychology is a new and different approach to the introductory course. The instructor is offered a series of short volumes, each a self-contained book on the special issues, methods, and content of a basic topic by a noted authority who is actively contributing to that particular field. And taken together, the volumes cover the full scope of psychological thought, research, and application.

The result is a series that offers the advantage of tremendous flexibility and scope. The teacher can choose the subjects he wants to emphasize and present them in the order he desires. And without necessarily sacrificing breadth, he can provide the student with a much fuller treatment of individual areas at the introductory level than is normally possible. If he does not have time to include all the volumes in his course, he can recommend the omitted ones as outside reading, thus covering the full range of psychological topics.

Psychologists are becoming increasingly aware of the importance of reaching the introductory student with high-quality, well-written, and stimulating material, material that highlights the continuing and exciting search for new knowledge. The Foundations of Modern Psychology Series is our attempt to place in the hands of instructors the best textbook tools for this purpose.

Contents

The Psychological Study
of School Learning

Whatever animal they study, be it earthworm or human being, most psychologists are interested in the phenomenon called learning, so they study the behavior of their subjects in an effort to understand this phenomenon. Similarly, most teachers study, in their own way, the behavior of their students in the hopes of understanding both the occurrence of learning and its failure to occur. It might appear that psychologists should be good teachers and that teachers should be good psychologists. On occasion this may be true yet often it is not. Why?

"Teachers do not use controlled scientific techniques,"

I

1

say the psychologists. "Psychologists set up artificial conditions unrelated to the realities of life in schools," say the teachers. Educational psychologists try to take the best from both worlds. Like all psychologists primarily interested in human behavior, they examine events in the lives of people, provide them with new experiences, and measure the behavior and changes in behavior that ensue. Their purpose is to describe and explain what changes can, might, and do occur in an individual as a result of his school experiences. Educational psychology differs from other approaches to the science of psychology only by virtue of its focus on the conditions, variables, and behavior commonly associated with education.

For the purposes of this book, education will mean formal schooling. So much of a person's learning takes place outside of school that without this restriction it would take little stretching of definitions to equate education with almost all of life and therefore with almost all of psychology. As the most massive and inclusive social enterprise of our time, formal education merits separate attention. About two million adults in this country work in this field, most of them as teachers, while about 50 million more people attend schools of one sort or another. Thus, more than a quarter of the population of the United States devotes a substantial portion of its time to education; most of these individuals may be called students, using the term somewhat loosely; with even less precision the remainder will be called educators.

The tasks of educators are many and varied, and although psychology has at least theoretical relevance to almost all of them, the topics presented in this book will be limited to those that directly concern student learning. Not only is learning the major business of schools, but it is also the central topic of psychology.

SCHOOL LEARNING

To many people the phrase "school learning" means reading, arithmetic, history, and the like. Psychologists prefer a broader view that includes changes in attitudes, values, ways of dealing with other people, and so on. Since what schooling should accomplish is a philosophical rather than psychological question, psychologists, in their role as scientists, study what schooling does accomplish and what it can accomplish, including undesirable as well as desirable outcomes. Typically a child enters school when he is five or six; ten, twelve, or sixteen years later his schooling is completed. During this time in school he will learn many things, not all of which are intended. He will acquire knowledge; it may be a knowledge of history or it may be knowledge that some particular response satisfies (or irritates) history teachers. The knowledge may or may not have that broad meaning to the individual we call understanding, but almost certainly a concomitant of this learning will be changes in attitudes toward the material studied (or presented), toward schools, school teachers, and perhaps toward other students. Furthermore, the individual's thinking and judgments will be influenced to some degree, large or small. Finally, all of these changes may contribute positively or negatively to the individual's personal and social adjustment. In short, schooling, even when narrowly defined, affects the student's personality, defined as narrowly or broadly as you please. To paraphrase two standard clichés, schools not only teach the whole child, they teach him something—willy-nilly.

These facts lead to such questions as: What conditions helped produce this learning? What conditions hindered learning or produced undesirable changes? Why doesn't more learning occur? Why don't students seem to make good use of many things they learn in school?

To answer these and the many possible similar questions it will be convenient to examine (1) the factors in school situations that influence and modify learning processes, (2) some of the major features of these learning processes, (3) instructional procedures, and (4) the effects of schooling. Discussion of the first two of these constitutes the major body of the materials in the chapters that follow, but a brief indication of the variables subsumed under these headings will be given here.

1. *Students and schools.* Since schools must deal with students as they are rather than as teachers would like them to be, the logical place to begin the study of school learning is with the characteristics of students. Their prior learning, their abilities, beliefs, and values play a dominant role in school learning. Schooling can change these characteristics—in fact, it usually does—but not all the changes are dramatic and in any case the relatively immediate goals of instruction must bow to these forces. No school can make a competent lawyer of a ten-year-old child in a year; in many cases it may be difficult to get him to understand even some aspects of the concept of justice. At the very least, student characteristics determine where instruction can begin and usually they influence both where and how far it can go. Chapter 2 is devoted to these topics.

Other factors in school situations that may modify learning processes are the organizational patterns and rules of schools, their teachers, the other students in the school, and the materials to be learned. It is in these areas that most of the arguments about education occur, perhaps because so many of these elements appear easy to change. A sample of the research on the factors in school environments that influence learning is seen in Chapter 3.

2. *Learning.* Chapter 4 contains a discussion of motivation, reinforcement, and transfer. These are standard topics in psychology and many aspects of them have been explored far more carefully in laboratory settings than in school settings since several types of research cannot be appropriately conducted in classrooms. In general, whenever sharp departures from normal conditions are required in order to rule out the influence of elements extraneous to the questions being investigated, there is no advantage in leaving the laboratory. When some unusual classroom condition is itself being studied, this may not be the case.

These restrictions mean only that the study of school learning cannot provide all the information needed to understand learning. They do not mean that one must study learning only under laboratory conditions nor that the often fascinating theoretical questions raised by laboratory studies of animal and human learning must remain beyond the purview of educational psychology. A few years ago, anxiety as a drive affecting school learning was almost entirely a matter of speculation; in recent years many studies of the role of anxiety levels in school learning have been reported. Similar progress may be anticipated on other topics, such as the role in learning of curiosity, exploratory drives, and the rewarding effects of stimulus complexity.

3. *Teaching.* The third step in the analysis of school learning is a consideration of instructional procedures. Although students do the learning—as most teachers would admit—it is not impossible to claim that students learn, or do not learn, regardless of, or in spite of, variations in the methods of instruction—as few teachers would admit. Nevertheless, no consideration of schooling would be complete without a discussion of teaching procedures, since on the face of the matter the way things are taught should be an important factor in learning. Furthermore, the discussion of teaching methods in Chapter 5 may clarify some of the dilemmas faced by educators in their attempts to use psychological knowledge.

4. *Outcomes.* The ending is the beginning; the characteristics of students are considered again in Chapter 6, this time viewed as consequences of school learning rather than as factors affecting it. Presumably, any learning that occurs in school has consequences, but Chapter 6 deals only with those changes in the individual's knowledge, attitudes, and abilities that are sufficiently important to play a prominent role in any future learning.

And so the circle is complete. The psychological traits of learners and the external elements in school situations together set limits and determine possible courses of learning. Several kinds of events occur in the process of learning, and teachers may intervene during these events as well as manipulate the initial conditions for learning. In any case, the result is a change in the individual that, if large enough and lasting enough, will appear in measurements of his characteristics. Because there is this circular aspect to the study of school learning, everything is related to everything else. The thread that ties all these chapters together is transfer of training.

TRANSFER OF TRAINING

When a student has learned something—call it A—he has changed so that when faced with the task of learning B, his behavior is often not what it would have been if B had come first. Attempts to assess the consequences of prior training on learning may be labelled studies of transfer of training.

To avoid confusion with the word learning, the term transfer will be used only when the transfer task (task B above) differs appreciably from the training task (the past learning, or task A) in one or more of its central features. Without this distinction, we could refer to the effect of yesterday's practice of A on today's practice of A as a transfer effect instead of learning. Practice of A can produce learning of A but usually its influence on the learning of B is less clear. For example, does learning educational psychology (task A) influence learning to teach (task B)? If so, is this transfer effect positive (helpful) or negative (harmful)? The common legal requirement that prospective teachers study the subject suggests that someone must believe there will be positive transfer. Adequate proof of the proposition is still lacking.

Reasonable but unverified convictions about transfer permeate educational doctrine and strongly influence not only course requirements but the daily routines of teachers. The study of parts of speech is assumed to facilitate learning to write well. Latin teachers have frequently claimed that a knowledge of Latin helps in learning French, Spanish, and even English. Because of the possibility of negative transfer effects, arithmetic teachers are often urged to avoid telling pupils that "5 subtract 7 can't be done," because many algebra teachers believe the years of hearing such statements explain the common difficulty students have with the addition and subtraction of negative numbers.

To understand transfer of training it is necessary to understand both the role of learning in intelligence and the role of intelligence in learning. The latter topic is considered in the next chapter.

Students

Whether he is called a pupil, a student, or even a person, each individual sitting in any classroom differs from every other such individual in ways that are related to what he learns there. E. C. Tolman once called these individual differences the H.A.T.E. variables: H for heredity or genetic differences, A for age or maturational factors, T for training or prior experience, E for any special endocrine, drug, or vitamin conditions.

Psychologists interested in learning have good reason for hating these variables. An experimenter is usually interested in the effects his procedures have on the per-

6

2

formance of his subjects, so the effects of the H.A.T.E. factors on performance are an extraneous nuisance. These effects can be so large that they hide the consequences of experimental treatments. The H.A.T.E. categories are perfectly sensible and reasonable, but because the forces they represent function simultaneously rather than separately in behavior, test scores do not reflect the effects of any one of the four separately. Therefore, it is necessary to investigate them as they appear in various combinations in measures of intelligence, personality, and achievement.

Furthermore, attempts to assess the relative importance of these various factors have been largely unsuccessful. For example, educational psychologists, along with many other psychologists, spent many years deeply involved in the so-called nature-nurture controversy. Although disagreements remain, it is now generally acknowledged that hereditary and environmental factors continuously influence each other (interact) throughout a person's life in complex ways. The manner in which they interact in infancy affects the manner in which they can influence each other during childhood, which in turn alters the possibilities of later interactions. In view of this fact, arguments about relative importance become absurd (see Anastasi, 1958).* To be sure, it is sometimes possible to indirectly assess the effects of one of these separate categories by manipulating or comparing groups that differ in some way, as when groups with different prior training are compared in order to assess transfer effects. However, it is particularly important to avoid assuming that IQ's, for instance, reflect only genetic differences or that achievement scores reflect only differences in learning. In both cases genetic factors interacting with training are involved.

Another important point to keep in mind is that when terms such as achievement, personality, or intelligence are used, some measurement procedure is implied, and these words refer to what the tests measure, not to something else. To discuss intelligence as something other than those things measured by intelligence tests can only lead to confusion. Consequently, determining what intelligence has to do with school learning becomes a matter for investigation and experimentation, not a matter of logical deduction from a definition of intelligence. The most common measures of school learning—achievement test scores, marks, and the like—should be treated in a similar fashion. In other words, what they measure must be determined by research. A score on an achievement test usually represents many things in addition to what the student has learned in a particular course; indeed, it represents the sum of all his related learning experiences, whenever and wherever they occurred in his life, interacting with his abilities and other characteristics. It is always fair to refer to such a score as a measure of performance, but only sometimes fair to refer to it as a measure of learning, especially when there is an implication that the learning took place at a particular time, such as during a given semester.

One of the most prominent features of any investigation of school learning is the wide variation in performance found among students, even within groups exposed to the same experiences. Some fourth grade students read

* Throughout the book parenthetical references such as this, giving author's name and year, refer to volumes listed in the Suggested Readings on pp. 115–116.

better than some high school seniors, while others perform at a first grade level; some high school seniors know more history than many college graduates; the fifth grade student who is more adept at arithmetic than his teacher is not unknown. The traits of individuals seem to play a major role in such varying performances, and an understanding of these individual differences can help one understand learning processes. Of these traits the most easily understood as forces in learning are those called abilities. Consequently, their role in learning will be examined before turning to the somewhat more subtle influences of the emotional and motivational aspects of personality.

ABILITY AND SCHOOL LEARNING

It is often assumed that students either do or do not have the ability to do certain school work and that this ability is essentially what we call intelligence. But brief reflection will suggest that there must be many partially different abilities, a number of which are related to the widespread differences in performance found in any school. After all, almost everyone finds ability differences within himself as he moves from one school subject to another. Psychologists have agreed for some time that intelligence has a number of different components, that these components are only partially independent of one another, and that an IQ represents a sort of crude average of several of these abilities. A consideration of the different kinds of ability will come later, since both historically and quantitatively the role of intelligence in school learning comes first.

Intelligence

Differences in intelligence among students, classes, and schools are more closely and consistently related to all kinds of school performance than any other kind of variable yet identified, be it motivation, the teacher's technique, or what have you. Virtually all measures of school performance—whether they are grades, scores on teachers' tests, or scores on standardized tests—show strong and stable relationships to IQ and other measures of academic aptitude. In large heterogeneous groups, that is, groups with wide ranges of scores on both measures, from one-half to two-thirds of the variations in school achievement appear to go hand in hand with the variations in intelligence, which is another way of saying that the correlations between these two scores are usually about .7 or .8.* In single classrooms and even single schools this relationship tends to be lower, because such groups are often somewhat more homogeneous on one or both measures; correlations as low as .3 and .4 are frequent although not typical. Table 1 lists IQ's and grade equivalent scores † on a reading test for 12 students drawn at random from 12 fourth grade classes in four different schools, and for 12 students all in one class at one of these schools. Note

* Correlation coefficients are not percentages. To estimate the percentage of agreement between correlated variables, square the coefficient. Thus, $r = .7$ implies about 50 per cent (.49) agreement.

† A grade equivalent score of 4.6 means that the individual is performing at the level of an "average" fourth grade student in the sixth month of the school year of ten months.

the greater range of scores in Group 1 and the increase in range after a year. Ranges will be even greater in the higher grades.

TABLE 1

Grade Equivalent Reading Scores at the Beginning of the Fourth and Fifth Grades

	Group I Drawn from 12 Classes in Four Schools				Group II Drawn from One Class in One School		
	Reading Score				Reading Score		
IQ	Fourth Grade	Fifth Grade	Gain	IQ	Fourth Grade	Fifth Grade	Gain
118	6.4	7.5	1.1	118	6.6	7.5	0.9
115	3.6	4.1	0.5	118	6.4	7.5	1.1
113	5.4	6.2	0.8	116	6.7	7.5	0.8
111	2.9	4.1	1.2	116	5.5	6.1	0.6
Average	4.6	5.5	0.9	Average	6.3	7.2	0.9
108	4.9	5.1	0.2	115	4.7	5.8	1.1
105	3.0	3.3	0.3	113	5.0	5.4	0.4
105	5.8	6.5	0.7	110	5.0	7.3	2.3
100	3.6	4.1	0.5	108	4.1	5.3	1.2
Average	4.3	4.7	0.4	Average	4.7	6.0	1.3
97	3.4	4.5	1.1	106	4.5	5.1	0.6
92	3.5	3.4	—0.1	98	4.1	4.8	0.7
91	3.1	3.7	0.6	98	3.1	3.5	0.4
81	1.3	1.7	0.4	77	4.0	6.6	2.6
Average	2.8	3.3	0.5	Average	3.9	5.0	1.1
Correlation with IQ	.70	.74	.42		.71	.35	—.01

These data illustrate the sort of relationships commonly found between achievement scores and ability scores. Intelligence measures can be used to predict achievement scores, although prior achievement in the same subject is frequently better, but in either case substantial departures from expectations will be found for some individuals. Grouping the scores in the table into thirds makes the regularity of the relationships more apparent, partly because means (averages) are more reliable (less influenced by chance factors) than individual scores. With big groups, great regularity can be obtained between the group averages, but the overlapping of the range of scores of these groups is consistently large (see Figure 1).

It should be apparent from Table 1 and Figure 1 that the relationship between the intelligence test scores and the achievement scores is much greater than is the relationship between the IQ's and the changes in those achievement scores. These changes represent what the students learned during

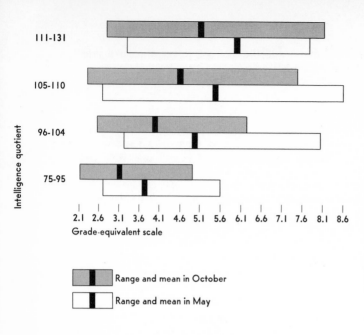

Intelligence quotient

111-131

105-110

96-104

75-95

2.1 2.6 3.1 3.6 4.1 4.6 5.1 5.6 6.1 6.6 7.1 7.6 8.1 8.6
Grade-equivalent scale

Range and mean in October

Range and mean in May

Figure 1. Fall and spring reading scores of 120 fourth grade children randomly selected from 12 classes. Scores were divided into 4 groups of 30 according to IQ's. Note the regularity of the means and the overlap of the ranges.

the course of a year. Since intelligence is frequently described as the ability to learn it may seem surprising that the relationship between IQ and these learning scores (changes) is so low.

One reason is the low reliability of measures of change, especially gain on tests. The average gain of Group 1 in Table 1 is 0.6 (six months), which represents a change from 50 items right to 59 right out of 120 items in the test. Chance fluctuations can be a large part of such small changes, and anything that fluctuates by chance cannot show regularity or a relationship to something else (except by chance). By including only items in the achievement test that most students could not answer before instruction began, J. W. Tilton found a moderate (about .5) correlation between IQ and learning.* Although these correlations are not as high as the .7 and .8 found between performance and intelligence in heterogeneous groups, the unreliability of gains does partly explain the discrepancy. Some other reasons will be mentioned in Chapters 4 and 5.

Thus, it appears that general intelligence tests may measure ability to learn to some degree. Nevertheless, finding a relationship between two variables does not demonstrate the reasons for it. One important reason why the correlation between measures of general achievement and intelligence can be so high is that some achievement batteries are constructed in a manner quite similar to that used in building general intelligence tests. A typical procedure is to assemble a panel composed of experts in each subject and teachers of the subject (these are not necessarily mutually exclusive categories) whose task is to specify the areas and topics that should be included along with their relative weights. Since these experts may have differences of opinion about what should be included, the items used tend to deal mostly with those areas

* J. W. Tilton. Intelligence test scores as indicative of ability to learn. *Educ. psychol. Measmt.*, 1949, 9, 291–296.

and topics agreed to be important. In other words, the material in these tests contains the basic core of the subject which is presumably common to the curriculum of most schools in the country. Thus, when individuals taking a test have had the amount of schooling for which the test is intended, most will have had an approximately equal opportunity to acquire the information being measured. A similar criterion is commonly used for items going into intelligence tests; that is, each individual for whom the test is designed theoretically has had approximately equal opportunity to learn the material included. Another common basis for selecting items is that they must be answered correctly by more older than younger children. This is perhaps the major requirement a test item must meet since mental age is the basic concept in an IQ.* This is not so important in achievement tests, but still, items that do not show improvement with increased schooling (and therefore with age) are usually discarded. So while the kinds of questions included may be somewhat more heterogeneous in an intelligence than in an achievement test, some of the essential features of the former are not too different from those of achievement test batteries.

General intelligence is strongly related to general measures of academic performance, whether they be grade point averages or scores on standardized achievement tests. But general intelligence has a low relationship to changes in these measures of general achievement, and thus prediction of learning on the basis of intelligence test scores over a short period of time, say under a year, is an extremly hazardous proposition. The improvement over chance in such predictions is so small as to suggest that one should not engage in such practice.

Ability to learn is part of what IQ tests measure but evidently this is not the whole story. Another typical way of studying the role of abilities in learning is to compare groups with different abilities. A brief look at some varieties of intellectual talent will serve to illustrate.

Intellectual Giftedness

For obscure reasons the term for very bright children is "gifted." The word "exceptional" refers to all categories of atypical children including all kinds of handicaps—for example, blindness, mental deficiency, emotional disturbance—as well as all kinds of talent; this odd terminology may be another reflection of the H.A.T.E. neurosis of psychologists and educators. A child labelled gifted usually is one who is above some cutting point on an intelligence test. The top 5 or 1 per cent, or perhaps those with IQ's above 130 or 140, are commonly chosen. Studies of such individuals have enlarged our understanding of the meaning of intelligence test scores and the educational correlates of differences on these scores. Although the volume of work on gifted children is very large, it will be sufficient to report some of what was learned from Lewis Terman's classic study of gifted children in California (Terman and Oden, 1948).

In 1921, Terman identified over 1500 children in the state in the top 1 per

---

* Thus, a mental age of eight represents the score of an average eight-year-old, but an exceptional score among six-year-olds. On this topic see L. E. Tyler. *Tests and measurements*. Englewood Cliffs, N. J.: Prentice-Hall, 1963.

cent in intelligence. Their mean IQ was 150, and the group included about 90 per cent of those in the state falling in the age and intelligence ranges studied. Identification was not always easy. When teachers were asked to point out their brightest students, they more often nominated the oldest students (who had the highest mental ages) than the brightest. It was found that approximately 16 per cent of those nominated by 6000 teachers were actually gifted. That is, in five out of six cases the teachers made a mistake. By simply selecting those who were the youngest in their classes it was possible to get more frequent success than by using teachers' nominations. This study occurred at a time when social promotion was less common than it is today and acceleration was more common, so that age differences in a class were usually greater then than now.

Comparisons of these children, when first identified, to a group representative of the population at large indicated that aside from being intellectually talented the gifted were generally superior on all counts—physically, emotionally, socially, and in adjustment, character, and home background. With respect to qualities related to intelligence, they were particularly high in memory, attention span, vocabulary, logical and critical thinking, power to generalize, common sense, originality, initiative, desire to know, alertness, and sense of humor.

When they were still in the elementary schools, this group was on the average accelerated about 14 per cent in grade for age. On the other hand, they were ahead about 44 per cent for age in mastery of the school curriculum. In fact, no clear relationship between school achievement and time spent in school could be found. For this group, amount of schooling and performance were not related, although intelligence and performance were.

Of major interest is the uneven school achievement of these children. It was highest in reading, languages, arithmetic reasoning, science, literature, and the arts. It was lowest in arithmetic computation, spelling, and factual information about history and civics. Generally speaking, a complementary pattern is to be found among those below average in intelligence: Retarded groups tend to be highest relative to their own average in just those subjects in which the gifted group tend to be lowest. This unevenness in achievement is in no way exceptional; variability is found among more average people also. Nevertheless, the gifted group is above average in all areas just as slow-learning groups tend to be below average in all areas.

This pattern of relative strengths and relative weaknesses is revealing. Consider reading and arithmetic reasoning in contrast to spelling and arithmetic computation. In what ways do the first pair differ from the second? Perhaps the clearest difference is that meaning and understanding play a more prominent role and rote learning a lesser role in the former than in the latter. Reading and arithmetic reasoning are developed abilities whereas spelling and computation are specific skills. The first two call for judgment, thought, and flexibility in behavior, but the latter two do not. Learning is often a part of reading but it would be difficult to claim that spelling a word is a learning activity of broad importance.

These then are the kinds of intellectual differences most clearly related to differences in intelligence. For in those areas where problems of transfer of training typically arise, measured intelligence appears to function with greatest effect. Transfer of learning in spelling and computation, however, is automatic since the behavior called for can become stereotyped with little loss. Note that both the latter are practiced so continuously that differences in ability to remember are minimized which also reduces difficulties in transfer since retention is a necessary condition for transfer. Both stereotyped behavior and poor memory are often characteristics of mentally retarded individuals.

It follows that measured intelligence is related most clearly to the aspects of school learning that rely heavily on a broad background of prior learning, the relevance of which varies from one time to the next. Furthermore, it is possible to change learning conditions so as to increase or decrease the importance of intelligence by decreasing or increasing the apparent relevance of previous learning or by altering the amount of preliminary training (see pp. 69–72). Another factor that can diminish the importance of intelligence in learning is a student's "creativity."

Creativity

The long efforts of psychologists to describe and categorize intellectual abilities have in recent years led to some helpful schemes and have made it possible to talk of creativity as a measurable entity. A way of categorizing the operations in intellectual processes devised by J. P. Guilford is shown in Table 2. Items measuring the abilities in the category of divergent thinking are not common in intelligence tests, which consist largely of items belonging to other categories.

TABLE 2

Operations Involved in Intellectual Processes

Operation	*General Description*	*Sample Tests*
Cognition	The processes in knowing, discovery, and recognition. Includes some reasoning.	Vocabulary, arithmetic reasoning, naming similarities between objects.
Memory	Retention of that which is cognized.	Memory span for number sequences, memory for word pairs.
Convergent thinking	Generation of new information from known and remembered information. Production of "right," "best," or conventional answers and solutions.	Completion of verbal analogies, arranging pictures in logical sequence.
Divergent thinking	Generation of new information from known and remembered information. Production of numerous, diverse, unusual, unconventional answers and solutions.	Listing objects with certain characteristics (Ideational Fluency). Writing captions for cartoons (Originality).
Evaluation	Deciding about adequacy, correctness, or goodness of what is remembered or produced by thinking.	Finding incongruities in pictures. Judging about identity of pairs of letter or number sequences (Perceptual Speed).

Adapted from J. P. Guilford. The three faces of intellect. *Amer. Psychol.,* 1959, 14, 469–479.

Tests that emphasize divergent thinking have come to be called tests of creativity. Although the appropriateness of the label is still in question, available evidence supports this usage; for example, adults of proven creativity tend to score high on such tests. On this basis, investigations of the role of measured creativity in school learning have been undertaken and have produced some consistent and striking results.

J. W. Getzels and P. W. Jackson reported one such study in 1962. Two groups of adolescents were drawn from a private school whose students were almost all from the kind of upper-middle-class homes that typically produce intellectually and academically superior students. All of one group was in the top fifth of the school in IQ but not in creativity; the reverse was true of the creative group, who nonetheless had high IQ's by usual standards. It should be noted that highly creative people are almost always of above average intelligence. In order to determine the meaning of the two kinds of measure, students high on both kinds were not studied. The 'IQ and achievement data for both groups and for the whole school are shown in Table 3.

TABLE 3

Total School Population versus High IQ
and High Creative Groups on Various Measures [a]

Measure	Total Population (n = 449)	HIQ (n = 28)	HC (n = 24)
IQ	132	150 [b]	127
School achievement	50	55 [b]	56 [b]
n Achievement scores	50	49	50
Teacher rating of desirability as student	10.2	11.2 [b]	10.5

Adapted from J. W. Getzels and P. W. Jackson. *Creativity and intelligence.* New York: Wiley, 1962, pp. 24, 29, 31.

[a] Comparisons of means.

[b] Differs from remainder of population at .01 or better.

When all members of one group have higher IQ's than those of another group as is the case here, the odds are extremely heavy that the former will also have the better academic record. Here the high IQ group (HIQ) is well above the school average in achievement but is not superior to the high creative (HC) group. Essentially the same result has been obtained in other schools serving less select populations. Hence, there is little doubt that the things measured by these tests of "creativity" have something to do with school learning.

Group HC can be called "overachievers," that is, individuals whose achievement scores substantially exceed expectations based on intelligence test scores (see pp. 29–31). Common explanations for overachievement are exceptionally strong academic motivation or especially favored treatment. Both of these possibilities can be rejected for this group. No difference in strength of motivation was found on either of two measures (results from one of them are shown in Table 3—the measure used is described on p. 19), and teachers preferred the HIQ group, not the HC group.

Failure to find differences in strength of motivation for achievement does not mean the two groups have the same attitudes and values—quite the contrary. Given a list of personal traits to choose from, the HIQ's preferred those qualities both groups saw as leading to adult success, qualities they both believed (probably accurately) teachers prefer. The HC's valued these qualities far less. The characteristic showing the greatest difference in ranked preference was sense of humor; HC's put this near the top of the list of qualities they would like to have, HIQ's near the bottom. Occupational aspirations also reflect differences, with HC's naming more, and more unusual, occupations. The HIQ's name mostly the traditional professions—medicine, law, and so forth.

These differences in values and attitudes of the two groups are paralleled by their written stories about pictures shown to them. The HC's do not limit themselves so much to conventional responses to the stimuli presented (they are not so "stimulus bound"); they use more humor and their stories have more overt aggression and violence in them (Table 4). When they were asked to draw a picture for a given title, analogous results were obtained.

TABLE 4

Percentages of HIQ and HC Groups in Certain Categories of Fantasy Production and Parental Variables

Category	HIQ	HC
I. Categorization of fantasy production		
A. From written responses to TAT pictures		
Having stimulus-free (nonliteral) theme	39	75 [a]
Presence of humor	25	71 [a]
Presence of violence	46	75
B. From drawings on a specified topic		
Stimulus free	14	50 [a]
Presence of humor	18	54 [a]
Presence of violence	4	35 [a]
II. Parental variables		
A. Education		
Number of fathers with college degrees	88	62
Number of mothers with graduate training	54	21 [a]
B. Occupation		
Number of fathers in business	17	46 [a]
Number of mothers employed	25	54
C. Attitudes of mother in interview		
Mentioned more than one unfavorable quality in child	43	11 [a]
Mentioned more than one criticism of school	70	37

Adapted from J. W. Getzels and P. W. Jackson. *Creativity and intelligence.* New York: Wiley, 1962, pp. 39, 47, 49, 62, 63, 64, 69, 70.

[a] Difference is significant at the .05 level or better. All other differences are significant at the .10 level.

These attitudinal, motivational, and emotional differences add up to two different ways of thinking, which we may call different "cognitive styles." These two styles are associated in two different ways with measures of convergent and divergent thinking but in the same way with quantitative measures of school achievement. So far as school learning is concerned the styles are equally effective, although why this should be is not clear. Perhaps the greater flexibility and imagination shown by the creative students promotes transfer just as much as do the aspects of intellectual functioning in which the high IQ subjects have the advantage.

It follows that intelligence tests measure only a portion of human intellectual ability and that other portions are also important in school learning. Also, the so-called nonintellectual aspects of personality—emotions, attitudes, motives—are part and parcel of differences in abilities and are not really separable from the intellectual aspects of personality even though it may be useful to treat them as though they were. Finally, when combined with other evidence, these data suggest that, although different schools are suited to different cognitive styles, the typical American school is more nearly suited to the HIQ group than to the HC group. Just as teachers prefer high IQ students, so school administrators rate teachers who show unusual ingenuity and originality less favorably than they rate teachers who are low on such measures. In addition, the correlation between students' scores on creativity tests and teachers' ratings of student creativity are slight. Teachers typically include under the heading "creative" the kind of thing intelligence tests measure and not what tests of divergent thinking measure. Teachers may not be able to identify gifted students very well, but apparently they can hardly identify creative students at all.

Getzels and Jackson identified two additional groups who were not high in IQ or creativity. One was a highly adjusted group, the other a highly moral group. Their mean IQ's were 125 and 127 respectively. On the achievement scale used in Table 3, the moral group had an average of about 52, while the adjusted group had a mean near 47. The IQ difference is negligible whereas the achievement difference is statistically significant. Here, in contrast to the creativity versus IQ approach, two groups identified by differences in attitudes were found to differ on an intellectual dimension. Further explorations of cognitive styles should prove helpful in relating personality variables to learning processes.

PERSONALITY VARIABLES RELATED TO SCHOOL LEARNING

Although the term personality may quite properly be taken to refer to the entire psychological structure of an individual, studies of personality traits and learning tend to focus on motivational patterns independent of, or unrelated to, ability. Treating motivation and ability as separate entities is universally recognized as potentially misleading unless it is clearly understood to be nothing more than a convenience. But convenient it is, since everything cannot be discussed at once and the area of personality is confusing enough by itself.

Learning situations arouse motives in varying degrees, but people also differ in ways that determine how strongly these motives become engaged at any given time. These differences may be variously described as differences in strength of drive, or need, or goal attraction. There may also be differences in the kind of motive aroused, as when two people work very hard at the same task—one because he wants recognition, the other to help the first.

Drives can be treated as rather general activating or energizing forces each of whose characteristic strength varies among individuals; some individuals are generally strongly motivated while others are not. One way of describing such differences in drive level is to call students unconcerned, anxious, or overanxious. This anxiety may be, but need not be, described as anxiety about something.

Needs are usually treated as more numerous but somewhat less general than drives, each need influencing a more restricted range of behavior. A student may be motivated by a need for achievement, a need for recognition, and so forth. The needs dominating student behavior may or may not lead to activity that produces school learning. Needs refer to goals almost by definition, but the goals involved are usually abstractions such as achievement or recognition. Another way of studying personality traits is to investigate a student's specific goals, such as getting an "A" in a course or on a test. Studies of level of aspiration examine this sort of goal-setting behavior.

The three variables just mentioned—anxiety, need for achievement, and level of aspiration—have been chosen for discussion because their relevance to school learning has been investigated as well as hypothesized, and because in this research some reasonably reliable measures have been used. No one claims these devices are more than moderately valid. A term like anxiety has almost as many definitions as there are psychologists who use it, but the number of anxiety tests is small. The result is similar to that in intelligence. Most people agree that ability tests don't really get at all those things we mean when we use the word intelligence in everyday conversation. But by common consent in research, the unmeasured components are called something else—divergent thinking, for example. Thus, in actual practice the tests have come to define intelligence, and research rather than definition is used to discover what intelligence is and how it functions.

Anxiety

In recent years the relationship between anxiety and learning has been a popular topic for research. Those who work in clinics with troubled people find excessive anxiety a common symptom. From this finding comes the popular view that anxiety is an indication of maladjustment and a cause of school failure. Generally speaking, however, in the research on learning, degree of anxiety has been considered an indication of general drive level, an indication of motive strength. A number of tests of general anxiety level have been developed and also some that refer only to particular situations, notably test situations. Commonly investigators use these tests to identify a high-anxious (HA) group and a low-anxious (LA) group who are then compared on some sort of performance.

Laboratory investigators have found that HA groups learn more readily than LA groups, but that this relationship is reversed for learning lists of paired adjectives. High-anxious individuals, in contrast to low-anxious ones, are progressively handicapped as a situation becomes more complex and as the number of possible choices among the responses increases. This is said to occur because high anxiety means a stronger drive leading to less variability in behavior and the more certain appearance of whatever has become the most probable response. Since in choice situations, before learning is complete, the dominant response is often incorrect, high anxiety is a handicap.

Working with elementary school children, S. B. Sarason and others (1960) found that in school situations matters are not quite so clear, perhaps because the characterization of these learning situations as simple or complex is not in itself a simple affair. Some aspects of school subjects favor the learning of HA groups, others that of the LA groups. Even problem-solving situations can be manipulated so as to favor first one then the other kind of student by changing not the content but what the student has to do. When there is no time pressure and when cautiousness and double checking are likely to be helpful, the HA student is given an advantage. When quick choices have to be made or when there is little chance to correct errors, the LA child has an advantage.

In general, measures of anxiety are not by themselves likely to be predictive of academic achievement. They should be more helpful in understanding the results of particular learning situations. Some schools, some classes, and some particular teachers are more anixety-arousing than others. Failure, for example, is an anxiety-arousing situation for most individuals, and some teachers keep the threat of failure dangling in front of the students. The belief that teachers enjoy doing so has not been fully verified. Failure and the expectation of failure have been found to handicap the test performance of individuals rated high on measures of test anxiety. Sarason and his colleagues report that among elementary school children test-anxiety scores are related to general-anxiety scores sufficiently to claim that the same general area is being explored, but the relationship is low enough (typically .4 to .6) to assert that there are important differences among people in the kind of situation that arouses anxiety. They found a negative correlation between test anxiety and both IQ and achievement scores, indicating that test anxiety may reduce test scores. The degree of effect increased from grade one to grade five.

It appears that anxiety level is an important variable in learning, and stable differences in anxiety among individuals exist. But unlike intelligence, whose relationship to performance is more nearly the same at all times and places and for all materials, anxiety has different relationships to performance and learning for different materials and different situations. High anxiety generally but not uniformly handicaps performance.

Need for Achievement

All motives have a direction and refer to some goal or some need within the individual. The Sarason group suggested that a child high on their measure of test anxiety has a strong need for achievement, from which it would follow that, for all but the brighter students, a strong need for achievement goes hand in hand with below average success in school. (The child could have instead a strong need to please the teacher—need for affiliation—or a strong need to avoid punishment or just a strong generalized fear of tests.)

On the other hand, D. C. McClelland and others (1953) who devised a measure of need for achievement, and report that scores have a positive relationship to achievement under many, but not all, conditions. The McClelland measure of n Achievement (need for achievement) is a way of scoring stories written about some of the Thematic Apperception Test (TAT) pictures * and has yielded some interesting if not entirely clear results. As noted, positive correlations (up to .50) have been found between scores on the n Achievement measure and both grades and achievement test scores. Scores on the test are fairly easily manipulated, being higher under conditions where achievement-orienting cues are prominent (for example, "We are measuring leadership ability") than under more relaxed conditions (for example, "We want to see if these tests mean anything"). The relationship to measures of achievement also changes when conditions are altered. Positive correlations appear to be more frequent when the achievement measure is concurrent with, or follows, the n Achievement test than when earlier achievement criteria are used. Instances of negative relationships between n Achievement scores and past but not future achievement have also been found.

Need for achievement is more specific than anxiety, and therefore a measure of the need should be more subject to situational influences. Anxiety may be aroused in a variety of situations involving a number of different needs, only some of which are linked to achievement motivation. Anxiety seems to bear roughly the same relationship to general measures of achievement that it does to specific measures of current academic performance. The same cannot be said of n Achievement scores, which are more likely to be related to some specific performance, particularly when achievement cues related to the performance are present when n Achievement is measured. That these TAT scores yield relationships to behavior that show substantial variation from situation to situation and from group to group can be taken to mean that the instrument is useless; but it also can be taken to mean that a single motive will influence behavior differently at different times and places and differently in different people because of variations in other functioning motives. The latter position seems more reasonable as well as more complicated than the former. In any case, there can be little doubt that the test measures some aspect of the values, attitudes, and emotions that influence school learning and performance.

The n Achievement measure is based on an indirect, projective test (one calling for responses to ambiguous stimuli), and the subject is unaware of the criteria to be used in evaluating his responses. More direct measures are often useful. Inventories and questionnaires that ask a subject about his attitudes and feelings toward school work often show substantial relationships to achievement. The Test Anxiety Scale for Children (TASC) developed by Sarason is an example. The obvious drawbacks are possible lying and lack of self-understanding. Lying can be partially controlled by checking for consistency of responses and by phrasing the questions so that the "right" answers are not obivous. Furthermore, students are not as dedicated to decep-

* Each picture shows one or two people in some not very clearly depicted place. The scene is intentionally ambiguous. The subjects' task is to tell what is happening, what led up to it, what is wanted, and how it will turn out.

tion and self-deception as some people believe. Carter's California Study Methods Survey (California Test Bureau), for example, contains a scale with the name Attitudes toward School that asks such questions as "Are you well satisfied with the grades you get?" and requires a yes or no answer. Among both high' school and college students this scale has yielded correlations with grade averages of about .5 and with achievement test scores of about .4. The relationship of the Attitudes scores to intelligence is well under these figures, indicating that the measure can make an independent contribution to the prediction of achievement.

Level of Aspiration

Some interesting results have been obtained through a related approach that deals with what is called level of aspiration (LOA). In a typical investigation of LOA, a subject is asked to predict his performance or state his goal before each trial on some task. Attention has centered on the discrepancy between the subject's stated expectations and his immediately prior performance (see Figure 2). The advantage of this approach lies in the direct relevance of the measure to goals defined by the situation in contrast to hypothetical and ill-defined needs and drives.

In some studies the task scores have been manipulated so that amount of "success" and "failure" can be controlled. Discrepancies between prior performance and goals set for the next task have proven responsive to such manipulation. Of interest here are the differences commonly found between students with extensive past histories of failure with the kinds of materials being used and those with a record of success. Failure groups usually exhibit widely variable and unstable patterns of discrepancy scores (expected achievement less prior achievement) for the experimental tasks, sometimes setting unreasonably high goals, sometimes choosing goals well below what they had already demonstrated they could do. In contrast success groups typically set consistent goals slightly above prior performance. LOA is fairly specific to sets of tasks and materials. A child with a record of success in reading and failure

Figure 2. Discrepancies between the previous grades and the grade aspirations of four students. Discrepancies are most clearly related to prior performance when the goal refers to performance on a specific task.

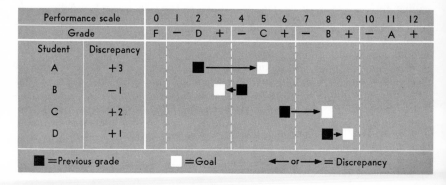

Performance scale		0	1	2	3	4	5	6	7	8	9	10	11	12
Grade		F	−	D	+	−	C	+	−	B	+	−	A	+
Student	Discrepancy													
A	+3													
B	−1													
C	+2													
D	+1													
■ =Previous grade		□ =Goal				← or → = Discrepancy								

in arithmetic will have small positive discrepancies for reading tasks and more variable and larger discrepancies for arithmetic tasks.*

Expectations about school grades are related to both past and future grades, and in some groups these levels of aspiration show considerable stability over periods of several years. Leonard Worell reported correlations of about .5 and .6 over a four-year period for college students' estimates of their possible, expected, and desired class standing. In this college, students are not told their grades but are told in which tenth of their class they fall in over-all average at the end of each year. Their estimates of what they could do if they worked up to capacity, less their estimates of their previous academic performance, were related to their actual grade averages, as were the discrepancies between their statements of reasonably satisfying performance and previous performance estimates.

Table 5 shows the correlations obtained by Worell. The more nearly the students thought their work was up to their capacity and the more nearly their standing was about what they called satisfactory, the higher their actual grades tended to be. When combined, the various discrepancies between the aspiration estimates actually had a closer correspondence to achievement than did aptitude measures (line 3 versus 4 in Table 5).

TABLE 5

Correlations between Grade Averages and Measures of Aspiration or Ability

Variables Correlated with Grade Average	Class			
	Freshman n = 138	Sophomore n = 79	Junior n = 85	Senior n = 75
Student estimates of their past performance subtracted from their estimates of				
(a) what they could do if worked up to capacity	−.63	−.70	−.57	−.35
(b) what they consider a reasonably satisfying performance	−.58	−.58	−.51	−.26
Combination of four discrepancy measures (multiple correlation)	.69	.79	.63	.39
High school achievement and aptitude (multiple correlation)	.47	.43	.23	.39
Combination of all variables	.72	.85	.66	.52

Adapted from L. Worell. Level of aspiration and academic success. *J. educ. Psychol.*, 1959, 50, 47–54.

In several other studies the relationship of LOA to grades has been very low, once differences in ability and prior performance have been accounted

* P. S. Sears. Levels of aspiration in academically successful and unsuccessful children. *J. abn. soc. Psychol.* 1940, 35, 498–536.

Students

21

for. Perhaps the spread of ability was greater so that the grades themselves reflected differences in ability more sharply than did the grades of Worell's group. That Worell's students knew only their gross over-all standing and that the discrepancy used was relative to their own estimates of past performance may also be relevant.

Personality Patterns

Each of these three approaches to personality influences on school learning has produced data worth attention. More data tying the three together would be helpful, but some interesting relationships are already apparent, two of which are noteworthy.

The first of these is the influence that success and failure have on both the measures of these personality characteristics and the relationship of these scores to performance. As was just noted success tends to stabilize LOA and successful individuals tend to set their goals just above prior achievement. Failure tends to make some individuals set their goals too high, but most will lower their aspirations after failure. Similarly n Achievement scores for some individuals increase after failure, others decrease; success may also alter the strength of the motive. Both experiences of and expectations of success or failure also influence the relationships between anxiety and performance. Given reason to anticipate difficulty or failure, HA subjects tend to do less well, while LA individuals tend to excel. Expectations of success reverse these trends. This common responsiveness to success and failure strongly suggests that meaningful relationships among the three can be worked out. The data on all three measures indicate that success or failure is a personal, subjective affair with marked individual differences in students' objectivity about their own performance.

Second, sex differences are very noticeable in studies of anxiety and in studies of n Achievement. Both the Sarason and McClelland groups found that their theories held true for most males but did not stand up well among females. These male psychologists seem to find the behavior of women awkward to explain. One might guess that the higher grades teachers give girls (girls' scores on achievement tests are *not* higher) is another consequence of males' misunderstanding of females. Unfortunately for this hypothesis, women teachers are particularly prone to give girls high grades although men join in this peculiar behavior. Sex differences have not played a prominent part in discussions of LOA, perhaps because no one has looked very hard for them or perhaps because direct questions about subject-defined goals conceal them. Concealing sex differences can make things less complicated, although it may also make them less interesting.

Many other ways of looking at personality in relation to school learning are common. Adjustment is one widely used concept because of the arguments about "life adjustment education," the publicity about mental health, and the conviction of many people that adjustment is a crucial variable in learning. This conviction stems in part from the obvious fact that emotionally disturbed children can be called maladjusted and many of them have serious learning difficulties, particularly in school. Also, as Terman found, gifted groups are above average in adjustment although less so than in achievement. Yet, some very clearly maladjusted and disturbed individuals do quite well academically, and, as noted earlier, highly adjusted students usually do not achieve academic distinction. The absence of agreement about criteria for adjustment makes these conflicts and those that arise with many other personality concepts more difficult to resolve than is the case where specific measures come into common use.

Complete personality patterns, including intellectual as well as motivational traits, are not really divisible into parts that separately influence the course of learning, nor are personality characteristics static, particularly among school children. Changes occur with age in the traits and abilities of a child. Some of the theories of cognitive development, such as that of Jean Piaget, make developmental patterns major determiners of what can be learned and what is learned in school at any given time. These theories and their supporting data are among the most significant developments of recent years but are too elaborate to present here.* One aspect of personality development, however, is too prominent in school learning to omit. It concerns the factors associated with a person's home and family—or, more generally, his cultural background.

CULTURAL DIFFERENCES IN RELATION TO SCHOOL LEARNING

The abilities, attitudes, interests, and values a child brings to school are a product of learning in large measure. Homes, neighborhoods, communities, and nations each have their unique culture or subculture. They each provide certain opportunities to learn and they exert pressure on the child to learn some things and not to learn others, even when opportunity is present. If collected in nations other than the United States, the kinds of data presented earlier would look somewhat different. The Sarason group, for example, found a higher correlation between test anxiety and general anxiety among American than British children. British children were higher on the test anxiety measure but not on the general anxiety measure.

Yet sex differences seem to be about the same, at least among Western nations. Girls tend to rate higher than boys in various aspects of language skill and lower in knowledge of and interest in mechanical and scientific matters. The role of socio-economic status also seems to be similar. On the other hand, American children seem to know more about science relative to their knowledge of mathematics than is true in most European countries. International comparisons on ability tests show only that there are cultural factors in these tests, since results often favor the country of origin of the test. Marked differences in personality patterns that are sometimes found among national groups are probably related to differences in patterns of school learning. Obviously, relative strengths and weaknesses can be decided only within the value framework of one country or culture.

In all cases one can expect tremendous overlap in the distributions of scores on any test of any two groups. For instance, children in the northeastern part

* For a good review of this area see P. H. Mussen. *The psychological development of the child*. Englewood Cliffs, N. J.: Prentice-Hall, 1963.

of the United States usually rank higher as a group than those from the Southeast on measures of achievement and ability when matched by age, sex, race, and social status. Yet one would have no difficulty in assembling large groups from each region for which this relation is reversed. The same is true for comparisons of groups differing in social status, race, age, sex, or any other basis of classification.

Family

A child's nationality, community, and position within the community are determined first by who his parents are. Some of the most visible influences on development are characteristic of those groups to which the family belongs. Intelligence quotients within a family are positively related. Parent-child correlations typically run around .5, as do those between children in the same family; school performance measures are similarly related. Gifted parents usually have bright or gifted children, and most gifted children come from families with other above average members. A similar pattern holds at the other end of the scale. Family influences on personality traits are strong, but they produce parent-child similarities less regularly than is the case with ability.

Table 4 (p. 15) indicates two of the many ways in which the parents of the HIQ children differed from the parents of the HC children in the Getzels and Jackson study. The psychological atmosphere in these homes differed noticeably, especially with respect to attitudes towards school behavior and achievement. Yet on external measures of social position and material wealth, the two groups of families were very much alike. Whether the parents of the creative children were themselves creative is not known.

Anxiety, especially as it bears on school achievement, has long been held to be a reflection of the pattern of child-rearing practices; middle-class children are supposed to be more anxious about school achievement than lower-class children. McClelland and his co-workers cite a positive correlation of .40 between n Achievement scores and parental severity as reported by 30 male college students. The authors argue from a number of facts that "achievement motivation in boys is associated with stress on independence training by their mothers." Similarly, educational and occupational aspiration are strongly influenced by parental views. For able high school students, the proportion hoping to go to college is twice as large among those whose parents want them to go as among those not so urged.

Socio-economic Status

Of the matters just mentioned, only the family's creativity lacks a visible relation to the family's social and economic standing in the community. The existence of social and economic hierarchies in American society is obvious to even the most casual observer. Whether the ranking is based on objectively measurable criteria such as parental occupation or on subjective ratings of social position by other members of a community, the relationship to school achievement and IQ is substantial. Table 6 shows the kind of relationships usually found between achievement, intelligence, and socio-economic status. Intelligence functions within social-class groups, and conversely social class functions within intelligence groups. The same sort of relationship appears when one compares intelligence scores of adults according to both the years of schooling they completed and their intelligence when they were in school (see Table 19).

TABLE 6

Reading Scores of 316 Fifth Grade Children Arranged by IQ and Socio-economic Status

	Socio-economic Status		
	Low	Middle	High
IQ Quartiles	Mean (n)	Mean (n)	Mean (n)
1 (110–129)	4.5 (6)	6.2 (34)	6.7 (40)
2 (103–109)	4.8 (18)	5.8 (22)	6.0 (38)
3 (92–103)	4.4 (58)	4.3 (12)	5.4 (8)
4 (70–92)	3.5 (62)	3.6 (16)	4.0 (2)

The matter of opportunity to learn is more important even within a single community than we sometimes like to acknowledge. In our society some groups are severely limited in their opportunities to learn many of the concepts and skills that are prerequisites for success in school; certain other groups have unique chances for such learning. These variations in opportunity come first from conditions in home and neighborhood, the greatest contrasts being between the suburban and slum areas of our large metropolitan districts. The schools to a large extent exemplify this contrast at least partly because schools tend to reflect the communities they serve.

The contrast in money available to the schools in a wealthy suburb and to the schools in a large city jolts one's notions of the meaning of equality of opportunity. The pedagogic tasks which confront the teachers in the slum schools are far more difficult than those which their colleagues in the wealthy suburbs face. Yet the expenditure per pupil in the wealthy suburban school is as high as $1,000 per year. The expenditure in a big city school is less than half that amount. An even more significant contrast is provided by looking at the school facilities and noting the size of the professional staff. In the suburbs there is likely to be a spacious modern school staffed by as many as 70 professionals per 1,000 pupils; in the slum one finds a crowded, often dilapidated and unattractive school staffed by 40 or fewer professionals per 1,000 pupils.*

The community and the school are inseparable. For example, I have walked through school corridors in slum areas and, looking into classrooms, have seen children asleep with their heads on their hands. Is this situation the result of poor teachers without either disciplinary control or teaching ability? No, the children asleep at their desks have been up all night with no place to sleep or else have been subject to incredibly violent family fights and horrors through the night.†

* J. B. Conant. *Slums and suburbs.* New York: McGraw-Hill, 1961, pp. 2–3.
† *Ibid.*, pp. 20–21.

For a while school may be a refuge and some learning occurs, but eventually, as a teacher quoted by Conant put it,

. . . the "street" takes over. In terms of schoolwork, progress ceases; indeed many pupils begin to go backward in their studies.! *

This progress, whether it ceases or not, is bound to be difficult for most of these children to achieve. Consider what they don't know when they start school that their suburban counterparts do. Naming colors, counting, and following directions are relatively unfamiliar tasks. Their vocabularies are one-half or less the size of the average for their age. They probably haven't owned a book and have rarely, if ever, been read to. This adds up to what teachers call not being "ready" to learn to read or do arithmetic. Their reading books in the first few grades commonly discuss life in a "typical" home: a separate house with a yard (in some cities slum children may never have seen a yard, much less known anybody who had a whole house of his own), two children, several pets, many toys, and a multitude of other things that put together are like a foreign land to them. Many of the ideas as well as objects are unfamiliar: taking a trip to the country in the family car, decorating their own bedroom, having a picnic, playing a game with "daddy," reading books for pleasure, having conversations about ideas, and so forth.†

Even if they learn to say the words in their readers, the meaning of what they read will be harder for them to understand than for the child to whom all this is familiar. Some people argue that reading about such homes is disturbing to children who do not have anything like what is depicted as normal. Be that as it may, initial progress is likely to be slow, parental expectations and help are meager, and teachers working in overcrowded, understaffed schools can scarcely be expected to pick up the pace. This conceptual deficit is accompanied quite obviously by emotional and attitudinal problems. Personality traits, including anxiety and aspiration levels, are typically of kinds that hamper educational progress. Data from almost all large cities show that as pupils get older, the gap in school achievement between middle-class children and those from "culturally-deprived" areas steadily widens. IQ's often show a corresponding decline. Nevertheless, the successes of the special compensatory programs under way in various parts of the country show that schools can arrest or even reverse this decline, even though they usually do not (see Chapter 6).

In recent years the worst slums in many cities have become identified as Negro ghettos. Since largely white slums show the same educational pattern and since middle-class Negro districts mostly do not, there is little reason to believe that this is basically a racial matter. The decline with age in relative intellectual and academic standing among rural southern Negroes suggests also that the problem is not confined to cities (see Table 7). Migrant workers and reservation Indians are additional examples indicating that this problem is neither just a Negro nor just an urban phenomenon.

* *Ibid.*, p. 21.
† In some respects a slum environment can be stimulating but the abilities thus developed are not typically valued outside the slum culture, and certainly not by educators.

TABLE 7

Reading Vocabulary and Reading Comprehension Scores
of White and Negro Students in a Southern State [a]

Grades	White		Negro		White-Negro Differences	
	Vocab.	Comp.	Vocab.	Comp.	Vocab.	Comp.
4	+3	+1	—8	—12	11	13
6	+2	—3	—22	—23	24	20
9	—6	—8	—37	—34	31	26
12	—15	—22	—51	—53	36	31

Adapted from B. Cooper. An analysis of the reading achievement of white and Negro pupils, in certain public schools of Georgia. *School Review,* in press.

[a] Mean deviations in grade equivalent scores from national median.

The existence of such large groups whose relative intellectual status declines during their school years deserves more attention than it gets from psychologists and educators. The reasons for it are less easily understood than many believe. For groups like those used in Table 7, mean reading scores correspond closely to mean IQ's if allowance is made for the increasing selectivity of the school population in the higher grades because of drop-outs. When the vocabulary scores are used, the white groups' averages drop from slightly above the fiftieth percentile of those in school to about the thirtieth percentile while the Negro groups' drop from about the thirtieth percentile to below the fifth percentile. In terms of IQ, this means that the white twelfth grade average is no more than one point below the fourth grade group whereas the Negro twelfth grade average is more than five IQ points below the Negro fourth grade group.

One might expect an increase in the achievement score difference but not in relative standing (percentile rank) and certainly not in IQ. Why then does this happen? Do intelligence tests given in the early grades overestimate what these individuals can do? Or does inadequate education create this situation? Much of the work on these questions has been done in the context of school desegregation.

School Desegregation

Critics of racial segregation in schools assert it is a factor in cultural deprivation because segregated school systems intensify and perpetuate the social and cultural disadvantage that is a part of life for most Negroes. Segregation by race as official school policy is unconstitutional, but *de facto* segregation still exists in many places, including areas outside of the South. In all likelihood, it will be many years before the process of desegregation is complete throughout the country. In the meantime, arguments about the educational and psychological merits of segregation and desegregation continue.

With respect to academic achievement, the most adequate as well as the most promising data come from the Washington, D.C. schools. The data in Table 8 show the improvement in achievement that occurred during the years immediately following desegregation. Other cities have reported little or no change in achievement. In one city the schools remaining all Negro turned in somewhat higher scores. In general desegregation has little immediate effect on achievement in and of itself. The Washington results seem to have occurred because of the strenuous efforts that followed the discovery of the very large deficit in achievement of the Negro pupils, the size of which had been concealed by the separate schools and different testing programs.

TABLE 8

Deviations of Washington, D.C. Medians from National Median
on Stanford Achievement Tests for Grades 3, 6, and 9 [a]

	Grade 3			Grade 6			Grade 9		
	Percentage	Deviation		Percentage	Deviation		Percentage	Deviation	
Year	Negro[b]	Greatest	Least	Negro[b]	Greatest	Least	Negro[b]	Greatest	Least
55–56	66	—9	—6	62	—12	—5	62	—18	—11
56–57	73	—7	—2	65	—6	—3	62	—19	—9
57–58	72	—6	—3	68	—6	0	64	—14	—5
58–59	79	—4	—3	72	—4	+1	67	—11	—5

Adapted from C. F. Hansen. The scholastic performances of Negro and white pupils in the integrated public schools of the District of Columbia. *Harv. educ. Rev.*, 1960, 30, 216–236.

[a] 1955–1956 through 1958–1959.
[b] Percentage of Negroes in each grade enrolled in the system.

Thus, desegregation is no panacea but it can improve the performance of Negro students by inspiring school reform. Throughout the country, wherever school systems have been segregated, Negro schools on the average have proved inferior to white schools on almost all counts. Typically, the school system spends less per pupil for the Negroes than for the whites. Equipment and buildings are inferior; libraries in particular show discrepancies in quality. For example, it has been common in segregated systems to buy new textbooks for the white schools and pass on the used, old textbooks to the Negro schools. Using 1958–59 data it was found that with Negroes making one third of the total school enrollment in Georgia, ". . . Negro school children and schools receive $37.00 per pupil less than white children in current expenditures, receive only one-fifth of the money spent for maintenance of school buildings, have fewer accredited schools . . . have only one-sixth of the state's library books, receive only 6% of the state's expenditure for higher education." *

This kind of discrimination is essentially analogous to that of slum schools

* Georgia Conference on Educational Opportunity. *Georgia's Divided Education.* Atlanta, 1960.

in nonsouthern states regardless of racial composition. In neither case is there necessarily any intentional malice. This is the way things are and changing them requires tremendous effort. It is no stroke-of-the-pen affair.

From these facts it can be inferred that inadequate education is one factor in the underachievement and declining IQ of culturally deprived children. For Negroes, segregation itself just as much as poor schools has been responsible, since for the bulk of this group the value of education has seemed obscure. Why finish high school, much less go to college, to become an unemployed janitor? Segregation has been the symbol for, as well as part of, the constellation of circumstances that has put Negro students at a disadvantage on every kind of measure considered in this chapter. Measures of intelligence, achievement, anxiety, n Achievement, level of aspiration, social class, economic status, and readiness all indicate the average Negro is likely to profit less from schooling than the average white child. These things all go together, and to have much effect the changes made must deal with more than one of these variables. A description of programs for producing such changes is given in Chapter 6.

Up to a point the attributes of children related to their school performance can be studied in isolation with profit. Beyond this point, as this section illustrates, interrelationships must be examined. Another kind of educational "problem," called underachievement, also illustrates this interdependence.

UNDERACHIEVEMENT AND OVERACHIEVEMENT

These terms refer to academic performance either well below or well above what should be expected on the basis of measured intelligence or aptitude. Often implicit in the use of these terms is the notion that intelligence alone determines achievement. On its face the term overachievement then sounds absurd, for it seems to mean performance better than the person is able to do. For this reason it is sometimes assumed that when a student with an IQ of 90 is getting straight A's, either the IQ is wrong or the grades are undeserved. This is of course possible. Logically the same reasoning could be applied to underachievement, but it is rarely done, perhaps because it is easier to imagine scoring lower than one should on an aptitude test than it is to imagine scoring higher.

Errors of measurement have something to do with these phenomena. If you test a group and then compare the top 10 per cent and the bottom 10 per cent on a retest, more of the top tenth will drop in score and more of the bottom tenth will gain. This shift is called statistical regression. It arises because the highest scores contain more positive than negative chance errors and the lowest scores more negative than positive chance errors. On a retest the high group will probably not be so lucky nor the low group so unlucky. Thus, cases of underachievement should occur more often among those labeled gifted and cases of overachievement should be more frequent among those labeled retarded. This is in fact the case, but the departures from expectation are too frequent and too large for this to be the whole story.

Something besides error must enter in. A discussion of underachievement and overachievement therefore becomes a consideration of the factors in learning other than intelligence. Some of them have been considered in the preceding pages. There are intellectual factors that influence performance not tapped by intelligence tests. Creativeness was the example given and highly creative students are overachievers. Almost certainly other abilities will be found to be important in academic performance. Underachievement has been most commonly ascribed to nonintellectual, motivational factors—anxiety, for one, although it does not function independently of intelligence any more than creativity can be divorced from its attitudinal character. The work with n Achievement scores and level of aspiration as well as that on anxiety emphasizes the importance of subjective feelings of success and failure. The data presented mostly indicate that these feelings are consequences of learning experiences, but they are also consistent with educators' conviction that unduly low aspiration levels are symptomatic of underachievement.

The personality factors that influence learning are themselves at least partly learned. Although immediate circumstances can alter motivation, it is evident that these forces are also consequences of long-term developmental sequences. A phenomenon like underachievement does not appear overnight. The data illustrated in Figure 3 show that the underachievement of both the boys and the girls developed over a period of several years in spite of the striking difference in the grade when underachievement began.

Intelligence is, if anything, even more a consequence of a long period of learning and is less subject to short-term changes, but it can and often does change over periods of several years. Readiness to learn involves both intellectual and motivational factors. A skillful teacher may on occasion be able to establish an emotional climate in the classroom that will speed a child's

Figure 3. History of achievement among male and female achievers and underachievers in two large high schools. All subjects had IQ's above 110 and had attended school only in the district. Achievers included all with above average achievement in grades 9, 10, and 11; underachievers included all with below average achievement in these grades. The mean IQ's did not differ. Significant differences in achievement began in grade 3 for boys and grade 9 for the girls. (From M. C. Shaw and J. T. McCuen. The onset of academic underachievement in bright children. J. educ. Psychol., 1960, 51, 103–108.)

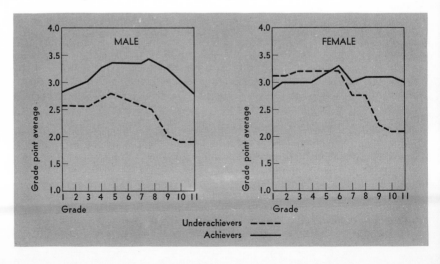

readiness to undertake some task, but if the student is not intellectually ready the teacher will have to plan a long sequence of experiences to ensure an adequate background of concepts and skills.

The primary feature of intelligence as it functions in school learning is the ability to identify and make use of the relevant aspects of previous learning. Since this calls for flexibility and adaptability, it seems probable that creativity influences learning in much the same way. One way of interpreting the role in learning of factors like anxiety is to say that they alter or modify this flexibility, that they mediate or intervene between the person's ability and his performance by modifying his interpretation of the situation confronting him.

Our attention up to now has centered on the personal characteristics of the learner. As the discussion of desegregation illustrates, the school can shape intellectual development; it too can modify a student's interpretation of new situations. Yet psychologists tend to treat differences among schools and teachers as far less important forces in learning than the students' own characteristics. That psychological research reflects this assessment can be seen by noting how much care is taken to allow for the variables discussed in this chapter and how rarely the particular school or classroom in which the subjects are found is considered important. The next chapter will show that this oversight can be serious, but that often it is not.

Schools, School Teachers, and School Subjects

The various characteristics just surveyed modify learning processes in important ways. They ought to; the individual is the one who is doing the learning. However, children are sent to schools in order to learn, and schools are meant to control and direct this learning. The next concern, then, is those features of schools that play a role or are meant to play a role in learning. These features may be put in three general categories, namely, (a) the school as an organization with varied policies, an administration, a student body, and a faculty; (b) individual teachers with sundry abilities and personalities; and (c) a variety of learning tasks

32

3

and school subjects that the individual learner must face and presumably try to master. These topics are still relatively virgin territory for investigation, yet they are so broad that only a sample of the work done and the problems to be studied can be given here.

The importance of differences among schools is not always obvious to the external observer; to the people who are responsible for schools—principals, superintendents, teachers, and so forth—just the opposite is true. To them the way they are doing things is the best way, or they would change, money and politics permitting. Whatever their reasons, school officials are inclined to use psychological arguments to justify many of their policies. For example, the traditional self-contained classroom has many proponents who believe it provides young children with needed security, but an increasing number of educators argue that the elementary school should be departmentalized much as high schools are because teachers cannot know everything. Other policies and practices on admission, promotion, marking, and grouping almost always lead to disagreements in elementary and secondary schools, as well as in colleges. Research has certainly provided no definitive answers about "best" practice. Yet the work done so far raises questions that merit attention.

School Entrance

When can a child most profitably begin formal schooling? The question involves the concepts of intellectual readiness and maturation. To make sense out of most of the research on this matter it is necessary to assume that children should learn to read in the first grade and that if they do not their time has been wasted. Two opposing viewpoints usually appear in discussions of entrance age. One is a sort of "children are little flowers" theory, which holds that the natural processes of maturation eventually lead to a physical and psychological state of readiness for learning. Instruction before this time is regarded as fruitless or very difficult. The second view holds that readiness is a reflection of learning (as opposed to maturation) and can therefore be produced at will by proper instruction.

At first glance, available information seems to favor strongly the first of these two positions. Children in the United States often show most rapid progress in reading about the time they reach a mental age of six-and-a-half. By a fortunate (or is it suspicious?) coincidence, most children reach this point while they are in the first grade. Any first grade teacher can show you that the pupils having the most trouble in learning to read are chiefly those with mental ages below the class average. To avoid such "failures," educators in the maturation camp suggest that children should not be admitted to school until their mental ages exceed six, until they are ready to "bloom." Yet in some countries reading instruction begins at age five, while in others age seven is most common. Reports indicate that relatively young children and those with the lower mental ages have analogous difficulties in these places

Schools,
Teachers,
and Subjects

33

too. But at least some children with chronological and mental ages under five can learn to read. Still, other things being equal, the older a child is when reading instruction begins, the more rapidly he will learn.

However, it is the less bright children who can show the most permanent effects of early instruction in reading. Children of average ability who learn to read early are likely to retain this advantage over their intellectual peers for some time, whereas bright children who learn to read early do not stay very far ahead of other equally bright children who begin somewhat later. The number of months or years spent in school seems to matter least among the bright students and most among the slow.

The data in Table 9 show the effect on achievement of variations in grade level and chronological age at different intelligence levels. Bright children older than their classmates do better by more than a year than equally bright children a year younger. The age effect among average children is less than a grade year (ten months). The bright child who is young in his grade does little better than the bright child of the same age a grade behind him (who is therefore older than *his* classmates). The grade effect is relatively large for the average children, however. Taken at face value, these latter data indicate that gifted children can postpone their formal education at little cost, whereas average and less bright children can profitably go to school early. However, these tests do not measure the broad sweep of knowledge that children may have acquired from their reading. Especially since bright children

TABLE 9

Effect of Age and Grade
on Expected Reading Achievement at Three IQ Levels

IQ	Age [a]	Grade	Expected Grade Score	Score Difference	Attributable to
130	9–9	4	6.7		
				1.2	Age
	8–9	4	5.5		
				0.1	Grade
	8–9	3	5.4		
110	9–9	4	5.1		
				0.8	Age
	8–9	4	4.3		
				0.4	Grade
	8–9	3	3.9		
90	9–9	4	3.8		
				0.4	Age
	8–9	4	3.4		
				0.5	Grade
	8–9	3	2.9		

Adapted from D. R. Green and S. V. Simmons. Chronological age and school entrance. *Elem. Schl. J.*, 1962, 63, 41–47.

[a] In years and months.

are likely to read widely, they may learn a great many things not measured by these tests, which may explain the positive findings for programs of acceleration. Bright children can keep up with older children of average ability, and consequently some schools admit gifted five-year-olds to the first grade. These children usually do well. Terman and Oden (1948) report that gifted children who graduate from high school before their age mates perform particularly well in college and thereafter. Both kinds of data suggest shortening the precollege schooling of gifted children.

It is, then, not a matter of when a child is able to learn to read, since any time after age three seems to be possible if an adult works at it hard enough, but rather of when the effort becomes sufficiently efficient to be profitable. How much more can a child learn about other things if he learns to read at age four than if he learns to read at age six? In any case, the kind of instruction, its purpose, and the circumstances under which the child is asked to learn matter more than absolute age. If he is above average in mental maturity, he will probably have relatively little trouble. If his mental age is well below that of the class, difficulty can be anticipated—presumably because the teacher's instruction is not suited to those who are at the lower mental ages and who are consequently less ready to learn under these particular circumstances.

An analogous effect can be found at any grade level. Children differ in their readiness to undertake any school learning. The less mentally mature will have more difficulty than those who are more mature and have had more experience relevant to the instruction they are encountering. These facts lead to the not very startling conclusion that instruction is most efficient when it begins at the point where the child is. Accomplishing this differentiated instruction in a class of 30, 40, or more pupils is another matter entirely. Promotion and grouping policies are supposed to help teachers meet this difficulty, just as school entrance requirements are sometimes fruitlessly manipulated for this purpose.

Promotion

Research has provided an apparently unequivocal conclusion about promotion from one grade to the next in the elementary school. Comparisons of regularly promoted students with those of equal intelligence who have been retained one or more times show the average achievement of the latter inferior to that of regularly promoted groups at any given grade or age level. The majority of retained students gain less their second year in the same grade than do otherwise comparable students who are promoted. The deficit persists thereafter and often increases. Moreover, those who have been held back one or more years in the elementary school are likely to become high school dropouts. Planned, if unpublicized, retention of certain groups of pupils to discourage their school attendance is not unknown and it works well.

Yet, to conclude that regular promotion is best for all students is not justified on the basis of these data. Promoted students in schools that hold back many are often stimulated by their success. Also, records of individual progress show that some pupils make no headway after promotion and some do remarkably well after being held back. One can either attribute these variations to chance (since the mean differences all run in the same direction), or assert that some students profit from being retained and others do not profit from being promoted.

Thus, these data are of practical use only to those who are looking for a mechanical rule of thumb. This rule would be regular "social" promotion for all. Of more interest are the unanswered questions about (a) the personality characteristics, if any, that differentiate pupils who apparently profit by retention (or promotion) from those who do not; (b) the differences, if any, to be found between the kinds of experiences these two groups have; and (c) why most "failing" students benefit from promotion. Intelligence does not seem to be a major factor but perhaps cognitive style is. Perhaps some children interpret retention as failure and others do not. Possibly anxiety level is relevant. It seems likely that putting a pupil through exactly the same routine he has previously failed will not prove very helpful.

Studies of acceleration, the opposite of retention, also show consistent results. Acceleration for the bright and gifted, especially when this is a planned speed-up, in contrast to grade skipping, has usually proved helpful. As always there are exceptions that educators cite when they reject this practice—which most of them do. Since most school administrators simultaneously accept the results of the studies of retention, a bias toward uniformity may be inferred. Yet children stubbornly remain different, as the next section illustrates more fully.

Grouping

All schools group students in some fashion, and only one-room schools can claim to be really heterogeneous. Age, sex, years of schooling, prior achievement, and measured ability are the more common bases of grouping. Any procedure based on only one criterion will produce groups still mixed on all other measures except those highly correlated with the one used. Age, mental age, and years of schooling are all closely related, particularly in schools that have age standards for admission and that practice regular promotion. Since these practices are widespread, most discussions of homogeneous grouping focus on the use of ability or achievement criteria within groups already similar in age and years of schooling.

In any class, the range in achievement levels in any subject is rarely less than four and often as much as eight grades. Thus, more homogeneity, the potential value of which has already been noted, would allow a teacher to use materials and procedures suited to the whole class. Therefore, the problems in instruction arising when one student has difficulty with fourth grade material and the next can read college texts supposedly vanish with appropriate grouping. This view is arrant nonsense. Students may perform at the same general level on an achievement test, but their knowledge of arithmetic will vary widely, as will their reading abilities, problem-solving skills, and attitudes toward the work, all of which may affect the outcome of any learning experience. Figure 4 illustrates the kind of "homogeneity" in reading one can expect from grouping by reading test scores. The lesson is simple: Some homogeneity in a group can be achieved on interrelated variables but substantial heterogeneity on other variables will remain; for people are not "homogeneous"

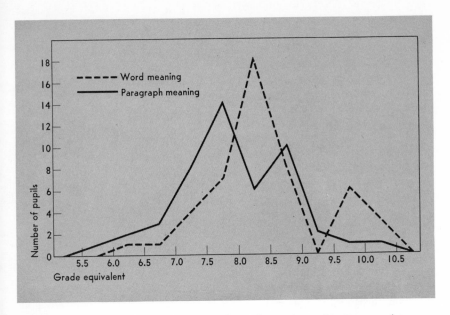

Figure 4. Distribution of paragraph and word meaning subtest scores for 48 seventh-grade pupils whose total reading scores all fell between 8.0 and 8.4. The group is very "homogeneous" in average reading ability. (Adapted from F. T. Tyler. Intraindividual variability. Individualizing Instruction, NSSE 61st Yearbook, Part I, Chapter X, Chicago: University of Chicago Press, 1962.)

within themselves. Note further that as time passes even homogeneity on the measure originally used to establish the groups will diminish.

It does not follow that grouping by ability or achievement or some other criterion is necessarily a foolish idea, inasmuch as other arguments may have merit. Not only may relative homogeneity in a few areas be helpful when the heterogeneity that goes with it is recognized, but differences in atmosphere are produced by interaction among the students. A few studies at the elementary level, for example, indicate that reading instruction in groups similar in general reading level but varied in grade level (for example, grades three through six in one group) can lead to achievement beyond expectations. Here the diversity of ages and other abilities may be a positive factor. The younger children, not outclassed in the immediate task, are provided with stimulation and models for growth; the older children have the satisfaction of exhibiting greater maturity and the challenge of keeping up with or ahead of the younger children, who are probably a bit brighter. The heterogeneity produced by homogeneous grouping can upon occasion be an asset.

At any rate, until a way of completely individualizing instruction is devised, grouping schemes of some sort are needed. At some point, diversity of achievement levels can become too great for a teacher to tolerate. Future researchers need to consider how grouping affects the influence of children

Schools,
Teachers,
and Subjects

on one another, since, as the work on entrance age and promotion suggests, the relation of a student's traits to those of others in his class seems to matter at least as much as the traits themselves. Without more knowledge about such effects, claims about "effective" grouping practices are ridiculous.

It is, in fact, not farfetched to say that aside from the administrative conveniences and problems associated with school policies little is known about most of them. Policies are a factor, but only one of several, in the "climate" of a school or class—that is, in the attitudes, values, and cognitive styles dominant in the group. Since people tend to conform to the norms and expectations of the groups with which they identify, this psychological environment mediates the influence of school policies on learning. Direct studies of such atmospheres appear to have promise for understanding differences between schools.

School Environment

The general psychological atmosphere of a school may depend on its students as much as on school policies. The anti-intellectualism typical of some schools is well-known. It can often be attributed to the attitudes of the student body and may exist in spite of counterattitudes of the faculty and administration (this disagreement is not always apparent).

An instrument called the College Characteristics Index (CCI) has been used to study the psychological environment of colleges as perceived by students and faculty. The test is based on the general framework used to study n Achievement; that is, there are internal forces called needs which are said to interact with external forces called environmental press to produce behavior. Parallel to the CCI which measures press is the Activities Index which measures the student needs corresponding to the categories of press. Achievement, deference, humanism, order, sex-prudery, and reflectiveness are sample categories. For example:

> . . . the need for order may be defined briefly as a prevailing trend toward the organization of the immediate physical environment and a preoccupation with neatness, orderliness, arrangement, and meticulous attention to detail. The magnitude of this need is inferred from the number of preferences a person indicates among such activities as "washing and polishing things like a car, silverware, or furniture," "keeping an accurate record of the money I spend," "arranging my clothes neatly before going to bed." The magnitude of the relevant press in a college environment is inferred from the number of respondents from the same institution who agree with such statements as: "in many classes students have assigned seats," "professors usually take attendance in class," "student papers and reports must be neat," etc.*

The categories fall into three general dimensions: impulse expression, dependency versus autonomy, and intellectual needs. A student's own pattern of needs is not necessarily related to his description of the environmental press, but mean needs scores and mean press scores of student groups tend to follow the same pattern in a college. Faculty perceptions of press

---

* G. G. Stern. Environments for learning. In N. Sanford (ed.). *The American college.* New York: Wiley, 1962, Chapter 21.

usually parallel those of the student body. Differences within, as well as between, institutions appear when student respondents are divided by major field, career plans, and the like.

For instance, in the college of one private university, faculty and students agree that a strong intellectual press is present. Both groups also agree that the college is nevertheless low on reflectiveness, that is, opportunity for discussion, evaluation, and individual creative activity—an area in which the "best" liberal arts colleges tend to be very high. The faculty of this school, however, see less press for student autonomy than do the students themselves, but at the same time they believe there is more press for intellectual open-mindedness than the students do. Apparently the faculty sees itself as taking supportive attitudes towards the students while trying to encourage independence of thought, but the students do not feel supported or encouraged to develop variant points of view. Would changes that shifted students' perceptions on these points nearer to those of the faculty also result in higher reflectiveness? It would be even more interesting to know if such changes would alter the effect of the college on the needs of these students and on their subsequent behavior.

Changes in needs do sometimes occur. In some colleges drawing largely from the upper middle class, seniors tend to score higher than freshmen on measures of impulse expression, whereas in institutions drawing lower-class and lower-middle-class students, the reverse has been found. Whether the changes are in fact the effect of the colleges on the students and whether there are real changes in subsequent behavior are both still under debate. Stern reports that, in certain liberal arts colleges, discrepancies between need and press are greater than in other kinds of institutions. These colleges ". . . are not so much unlike their students as they are ahead of them, being characterized by a built-in strain toward high intellectual achievement and personal autonomy which is present in their students, but to a far lesser degree." * Possibly a college environment which students perceive as containing a strong press for independence is associated with increases in levels of aspiration for further academic training. This might explain why the private liberal arts colleges of high prestige, which stand out on measures of this kind of press, produce an exceptionally large number of those who get Ph.D.'s in science.

Much excitement was generated some years ago by the discovery of the high "productivity" of these institutions (number of Ph.D.'s per 1000 students) in the field of science. Many of the schools did not have football teams and/or fraternities, and they were mostly coeducational, private, non-denominational, small, non-Southern, and so forth. The feature emphasized in the descriptions depended somewhat on the preferences of the writer. Institutions with other characteristics were found to have high rates of productivity in other areas—for instance, the humanities or the social sciences. Unfortunately it was later found that, when adjusted for the abilities of entering students, the productivity ratings of these institutions were no longer exceptional; the students were, the institutions were not—end of excitement.

One thing is clear—good students, good faculties, and certain atmospheres tend to go together. The characteristics of a topnotch technical school will

* *Ibid.*, p. 719.

differ from those of a prestigious liberal arts college, but both will also differ from the less productive institutions of their own kind, and these latter differences are closely related to the abilities of the student body. Indeed, these differences can be so large that the average achievement test scores of entering freshmen at one college may exceed the average of graduating seniors at another.

Just because able students tend to enroll in the "better" schools which have the "better" faculties, even in the public elementary and secondary schools, it does not follow that student intelligence determines these conditions. It is hard to believe that the qualities of a school faculty, quite apart from student characteristics, are unimportant, but research on teacher characteristics does not clearly support that thesis. The reasons why are worth exploring.

SCHOOL TEACHERS

Teacher competence has been the subject of intensive investigation for years—over 400 quantitative studies done between 1910 and 1950 are known and the pace has increased since then. The amount of armchair analysis is larger still. The studies in this area probably typify educational research as fully as the work in any other area. A good bit of it has been both methodologically and psychologically naive. But, although results remain meager, improvement in quality has been steady, as investigators learn what questions to ask and how to ask them. It is this last aspect of the topic, not the information acquired as such, that deserves emphasis. The work done falls under three general, albeit related, headings: the characteristics of teachers' classroom behavior, the measurement of teacher competence, and the prediction of teacher success. Since this logical order reverses the pattern research has tended to follow, the last of these will be considered first.

Prediction of Teacher Success

Prediction calls for some sort of measurement yielding scores (or ratings, or categories) from which the prediction can be made. Such a measure, regardless of form, may be called a test. When the test scores of a group of individuals show a non-chance relationship, typically a positive correlation, to their scores on another measure taken later, predictive validity for the first test may be claimed. The characteristics of the second measure, commonly called the criterion measure, are as important as those of the first test. It is the difficulties with criterion measures that have largely defeated attempts to predict teacher success.

The preceding statement suggests that no adequate measure of teacher competence has been devised. At this point many teachers, principals, and supervisors, to say nothing of students and parents, are likely to say, "Nonsense. I can tell a good teacher from a bad one even if you can't." This conviction has led to many investigations using ratings by either supervisory personnel, students, outside observers, or other teachers. The ratings used vary widely. In some studies principals or supervisors have been merely asked to indicate their best and poorest teachers. In other cases someone may rank teachers in order of general merit. More elaborate schemes may call for assigning numerical weights to each of a series of items or categories which themselves may vary in specificity. Thus, "Does he understand his pupils?" or "Is time wasted getting class started?" may be answered yes or no or scored on a five-point scale from "Poor" to "Excellent." Various numerical "scores" may then be devised. These rating procedures can become exceedingly elaborate. Bias, subjectivity, and lack of reliability often plague any kind of research based on ratings, and the teacher-ability studies are no exception, although care and foresight can do much to mitigate these difficulties.

One of the most important determinants of teacher ratings is the relationship between the rater and the teacher being rated. Supervisors' ratings, students' ratings, self-ratings, and ratings by outside observers often disagree. Personality factors exhibited in relationships with other adults influence the ratings of the teacher by principals and other supervisory personnel. Thus friendliness, considerateness, personal warmth, cooperativeness, need for affiliation, and the like often appear to be factors. Warmth and friendliness also influence students' ratings of their teachers, but since some teachers have relationships with students different from their relationships with adults, correlations among ratings made by different groups may be low.

Such findings have not convinced one and all that ratings are useless as criterion measures. Tests used to predict ratings include, either singly or in combination, intelligence tests, achievement tests, high school and college grades, number of education courses, age, experience, attitudes toward and interest in teaching, and sundry personality and attitude tests. Taken alone no single one of these variables predicts judgments of competence very well. Perhaps an appropriate combination would do so but that combination is still unidentified.

Logically, some degree of intelligence must be a necessary condition for success, however measured. Since mentally retarded individuals rarely become teachers, regardless of what students may think, it may be that the low and inconsistent relationships between measured intelligence and success reflect the rarity of teachers' falling below the point where intelligence becomes crucial. Yet not only has intelligence been significantly correlated with ratings in some studies, but also in a variety of investigations, such related measures as grade point average from all courses or from professional courses, highest degree held, and knowledge of material being taught have appeared to be relevant. More often than not, at least one of the set of such measures used in a given study yields a low-to-moderate nonchance correlation, say between .3 and .5. But no single measure can be counted on. The variations may depend on the circumstances under which the teacher is working, the students, and materials he must handle. The tendency for intelligence to be more of a factor in ratings of high school teachers than in ratings of elementary school teachers supports this notion.

The use of measures not originally designed to predict teaching effectiveness is another part of the difficulty. Tests like the National Teacher Examination, however, gauge professional knowledge, general intelligence, and knowledge of subject matter, and these are the logical foundations of teacher success. Yet scores on this test have not been shown to be related to ratings either.

At this point, most psychologists would point to the criterion ratings as the most probable immediate source of confusion. Perhaps ratings introduce irrelevant factors; perhaps all of us, educators and students alike, are so full of superstition and misinformation about learning that we can't tell a good teacher from a poor one no matter how we proceed. Or, again, perhaps it doesn't really matter who does the teaching—a theory a number of school boards apparently espouse. If any of these suggestions were true, prediction would be nearly impossible. Consequently, a closer look at the attempts to measure teacher effectiveness is needed.

Teacher Effectiveness

Few people disagree with the notion that the "effective" teacher is one who produces desirable changes —for example, learning in pupils. Ratings then are appropriate criterion measures of predictors only if they themselves are related to pupil change; they should at least have what is called concurrent, as opposed to predictive, validity. The difference is simply one of timing. The concurrent validity of a test is indicated by its correlation with the criterion measure, both measures being taken pretty much at the same time; measures of traits and characteristics that change easily during a period of time may have high concurrent validity but no predictive validity.

The logical criterion measures for teacher ratings are measures of pupil learning. Since changes in students' achievement test scores usually have low relationships to pretest scores (see Table 1), mean class gains on various tests might offer reasonable evidence of teacher effectiveness, particularly if allowances are made for student intelligence. Adjustments can be made for as many variables as appear important. Such adjusted changes have been called residual pupil gain. Unfortunately, direct attempts to predict pupil gain, adjusted or not, from teacher measures have yielded results much like the attempts to predict ratings. Intellectual factors, for example, often appear related to residual pupil gain, but in an inconsistent fashion. This similarity to teacher ratings with respect to correlating with other measures does not mean that pupil gain is related to ratings. In fact, the one clear unequivocal fact to emerge from these investigations is that whatever it is ratings of teachers measure, it does not include pupil learning. Teacher ratings are not positively related to pupil gain, they are not negatively related to pupil gain, they are unrelated to pupil gain.

Moreover, logical though it may seem, attempting to find measures of teacher behavior that have predictive or concurrent validity for student learning is not entirely sensible. What a student learns while he is in some class (from the teacher?) is partly a function of what he has learned in the past and what he is currently learning elsewhere. To assign responsibility for change to a single adult in the student's environment is probably unrealistic in most cases. Even more to the point is the likelihood that some teachers are more effective than others for only some students and for only some purposes. Validity coefficients—that is, correlations between tests and criteria—apply to given situations and given populations. It is quite probable that teaching situations vary in several significant ways, and it is certain that among the nearly two million teachers in the United States great diversity can be found. These variations are multiplied by differences among students. For such a large scale enterprise as the assessment of teaching effectiveness, an attack based on the concepts of predictive and concurrent test validity is far too limited. The increasingly widespread recognition of these limitations represents a large step forward.

Simple test-criterion relationships are unlikely to be found even if satisfactory criterion measures are developed, since teacher behavior is only one of the variables in student learning all of which probably interact with one another. A few, notably pupil intelligence, are of such importance that their influence is not usually masked by the others, such as teacher personality, teaching methods, materials, class and school characteristics, and so on. The available evidence strongly suggests that under normal circumstances teacher variables are not that powerful, and even more elaborate studies controlling more of these nonteacher variables will prove to be of little value.

Differences among teachers can be important only because they affect the functioning of other elements in learning. Suppose two teachers scored quite differently on Test X. They are using the same set of spelling materials in generally similar eighth grade classes; a multiple choice test shows about a third of the students in each class making scant progress in spelling, but Teacher A's "failures" are largely among the higher scorers on a measure of test anxiety whereas Teacher B's are representative of all students on the anxiety measure. Now suppose Test X led to the use of the anxiety scale because the theory on which Test X was based suggested that individuals with scores similar to B's tend to perform in a manner which should reduce the level of anxiety among more anxious students. This reduction should help highly anxious students with tests requiring difficult discriminations, such as the choice between comitee, commitee, committee, and comittee.

If the preceding were not just fantasy, we could say that the theory was pretty good and that the teacher measure (Test X) offered information about probable teacher effectiveness. Confirmation of a variety of inferences of this sort would increase confidence in the meaning of the scores of teachers. Eventually Test X could be labeled a valid measure of teacher effectiveness, not because it directly correlates with a criterion measure, but because it yields scores whose meaning for effectiveness is known. Validity of this sort is called construct validity.

Test X would have no validity as defined by the predictive or concurrent procedures. By adding a theory that successfully explains the relationships among the variables involved it becomes possible to see the indirect influence of teacher behavior. Thus, it becomes necessary to identify the attributes of teachers that may appear in their classroom behavior.

Teacher Characteristics

To find instruments to measure the attributes of people in their role as teachers, this time without reference to effects on students, it is possible to make some use of the kind of material already discussed. For example, attempts to validate the Minnesota

Teacher Attitude Inventory (MTAI) against ratings of effectiveness indicate that the test measures something fairly stable in teacher behavior, even though a relationship to pupil behavior has not been established. The MTAI, designed to predict teacher-pupil rapport, is, in fact, related to ratings of competence chiefly when the rater is instructed to consider this rapport. The test is based on the traditional idea that teachers should "understand" their students, meaning that the teacher should be a warm, friendly, sympathetic, and somewhat permissive individual in his dealings with students. This view is particularly common among people involved in teacher education. (The accusation that we substitute understanding for content in education courses is refuted by the fact that warmth toward students is no more evident in education departments than elsewhere.) It is more representative of the views of people in elementary education than those in secondary education. As expected, then, scores tend to rise among students taking education courses, drop somewhat after teaching experience, and are typically higher among elementary than secondary school teachers. College students instructed to fake either permissive or authoritarian attitudes generally get higher and lower scores, respectively, than students given standard instructions. This last result creates doubts about the practical usefulness of the MTAI even for research purposes, but, like the other results, is positive, albeit indirect, evidence that it has construct validity as a measure of a commonly observed dimension of teacher behavior.

This dimension has appeared in a number of studies, many of them not using the MTAI. It involves observable patterns of classroom behavior and is crudely predictable from attitude and opinion inventories. This "warm-cold" dimension of teacher behavior is similar to one of the three patterns identified in an extensive series of studies reported by D. G. Ryans. They are described in Table 10.

These dimensions are largely independent of one another among secondary teachers of academic subjects but closely related among elementary teachers. It is possible to identify teachers who are stimulating and businesslike in the classroom but whose relationships with students show little warmth. Thus, even if one divided teachers into only high and low groups at the median of these three dimensions, eight different combinations are possible. These combinations might be called teaching styles. The partial interdependence of the dimensions means that some of these eight styles will appear more often than the others.

Although it seems unreasonable to believe that a dull, slipshod, aloof teacher can be very effective, apparently these styles of teaching do not determine effectiveness. Nevertheless, they describe the way teachers play their role and reflect teachers' attitudes toward their task. At this point evidence ceases and if, in spite of the largely negative evidence, one wishes to discuss the influence of teacher personality on students, it is necessary to to turn to speculation. The following hypotheses seem worth exploring:

1. Teacher personality—their abilities, attitudes, and values—in conjunction with the environmental press *on the teachers,* determines teaching style (and possibly method as well).

2. The style of a given teacher is one factor influencing the environmental

TABLE 10

Characteristics of Elementary and Secondary School Teachers

Patterns of Observed Teacher Behavior in the Classroom	Teacher Response Measures (Paper and Pencil) Most Closely Related to Observed Patterns
Pattern X	Measures Related to Pattern X
Warm, understanding, friendly versus Aloof, egocentric, restricted	1. Tendency to choose the more friendly, understanding activities 2. Amount of permissiveness favored (elementary teachers only) 3. Tendency to choose the more stimulating activities 4. Verbal understanding 5. Emotional stability or adjustment 6. Tendency to have favorable opinions of pupils (secondary teachers only)
Pattern Y	Measure Related to Pattern Y
Responsible, businesslike, systematic versus Evading, unplanned, slipshod	1. Tendency to choose the more businesslike, systematic activities
Pattern Z	Measure Related to Pattern Z
Stimulating, imaginative, surgent versus Dull, routine	1. Tendency to choose the more stimulating activities

Adapted from D. G. Ryans. *Characteristics of teachers.* Washington, D. C.: American Council on Education, 1960.

press perceived *by students.* Especially beyond the elementary school this influence is probably small.

3. Common elements in the styles of a faculty taken as a group probably can have much stronger effects on the school environment, but since schools tend to hire teachers with styles that reinforce the existing press pattern, this force is often just one of several working in the same direction (administration, student body, and community characteristics). Teachers probably seek this kind of compatability.

4. A given teacher, then, will change a given student's achievement and personality development only if his teaching style alters the press felt by the student. The student's personality determines what sort of change this will be.

It is a fair guess that homogeneity of teaching style in a faculty will prove undesirable. Perhaps some day schools will deliberately try to assemble faculty groups with a spread of styles just as some colleges now try to construct classes of entering students with diverse backgrounds, interests, and abilities. Unfortunately, the most efficient way to assess these hypotheses and

Schools,
Teachers,
and Subjects

45

proposals would be to experiment, and the prospects of persuading any school system to deliberately manipulate the faculties of its schools for such a purpose seem remote.

Educators have been little more willing to experiment with what is taught in schools than with who does the teaching, although unevaluated changes are common, perhaps because such experiments always raise the nasty problem of what students should learn. There are, however, differences among learning tasks quite aside from any differences in value. As was noted earlier, the nature of a task determines the effect of anxiety on learning. Thus, it is necessary to examine the characteristics of learning tasks in school subjects. Do the various subjects have psychologically different learning tasks? Is it true that some subjects are inherently more difficult than others? Do differences in ability affect learning more in some subjects than in others? To what extent do learning tasks impose limitations on the procedures and processes of learning?

To answer such questions some categories are needed. At this point psychologists and educators tend to part company; the latter use school subjects, whereas the former more often than not use a variety of other categories that usually stress either the inferred nature of the learning process involved (for example, conditioning, problem-solving, rote learning) or the nature of the response (for instance, motor skills, verbal learning). These categories cut across subject matter lines and do not refer to content. Those that do refer to content are commonly laboratory tasks (such as mazes, paired associates, mirror tracing). The task variables usually studied by psychologists include length, difficulty, complexity, sequence, organization, familiarity, and meaningfulness, all of which are interrelated.* A large proportion of this work has been done with relatively meaningless materials, however.

This does not necessarily mean that categorization by school subject is inappropriate, but it does mean that, with the exception of reading and possibly arithmetic, there is no really substantial body of data about the learning of a particular school subject. Therefore, one cannot make the comparisons needed to develop generalizations about the influence of subjects on learning.

The only variable that seems to be really useful at present is amount of meaning. An examination of the role of meaning in learning will make it possible to speculate about what the organized nature of a school subject has to do with the learning of it. The importance of meaning in classroom learning is easily illustrated. A Shakespearean play is certainly potentially full of meaning. Yet many high school students who study Shakespeare do not understand what they are reading and get very little meaning from the material. Consequently about the only thing they remember is the difficulty and boredom, perhaps because feelings mean something to the individual.

A great deal of the material to be learned in school, whether in history,

* The specific sensory attributes of stimulus materials—vividness of color, shape, tone and so on—form another relevant type of category, but will be ignored here.

Schools,
Teachers,
and Subjects

46

arithmetic, grammar, or science, can be classified as information or facts. Such material can be readily learned by rote and often is, with the consequence that only those portions of it extensively practiced are likely to be retained. And in actuality, many facts a student acquires in school at all levels from elementary school through college are really forgotten rather quickly, as Figure 5 suggests. Tests given to college students a year after they have taken a college course typically show a performance that is at best 50 per cent as good as what they could do at the end of the course. One might infer that a great deal of time in schools and colleges is wasted in having students learn facts so promptly forgotten. The popularity of this view is not a measure of its merit. Without learning facts to back them up, generalizations are forgotten just as easily, probably because they then have little meaning. Furthermore, there is reason to believe that the transfer effects of learning do not dissipate anywhere near as rapidly as the curves of forgetting in Figure 5 might suggest.*

Sometimes content that has little meaning to the student is learned as thoroughly in school as something rich in meaning, but under these circumstances the two will differ in how they are learned. Learning tasks are variable factors in learning because of their differences in meaning to stu-

* M. E. Bunch. The amount of transfer in rational learning as a function of time. *J. comp. Psychol.*, 1936, 22, 325–337.

Figure 5. Curves of retention when the amount retained is expressed as a percentage of amount learned. Retention by the fifth grade children of geographical information learned from reading. Even after taking the test twice before, performance was down 25 per cent in two months. (Adapted from H. R. Tiedeman. A study in retention of classroom learning. J. educ. Res., 1948, 42, 516–531.)

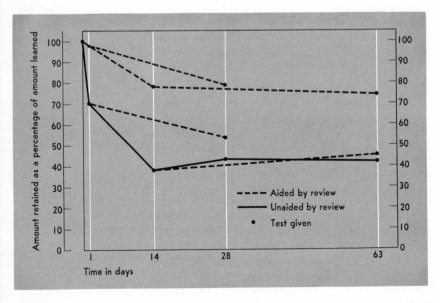

dents. If students were not so eager to memorize instead of trying to understand, it would be superfluous to explore this somewhat less than obscure point further. But since, one way or another, many people learn to try memorization first, it is appropriate, before discussing meaning, to consider rote learning—that is, learning in which meaning is not important.

Rote Learning

Some school materials call for rote learning by their nature or for convenience—for example, names, dates, number facts, and all the symbols, signs, and conventions used for the sake of brevity and simplicity. Other materials (geometric proofs, for example) do not require rote memorization but can be learned almost entirely without meaning if an individual so chooses; however, retention and transfer thereby become more difficult. Strictly speaking, meaning plays no role in rote learning, and understanding is not relevant. Yet an examination of research on rote learning shows that it is difficult to make meaning irrelevant.

The most obvious influence on the ease of rote learning is the amount or length of material. The more there is to learn, the harder it is to learn it. Somewhere between six and ten digits or unrelated words can be learned (and quickly forgotten) by most adults from one presentation. This immediate memory span is related to age and is an ability included in many intelligence tests. Both span and retention are increased when items are connected, as in a prose passage or poem. This is easily verified. Virtually anyone given a list of, say, five words can learn it at least temporarily from one reading. The same person given a list of 20 unrelated words (take the first word in each of 20 lines on this page) will find it takes a substantial period of time (that is, a number of repetitions) to learn, even if the list is broken into four sets of five words, each of which could be learned at one reading. If the words are connected in a sentence, like this one, both rate of learning and retention will be increased.

There are a number of devices that can facilitate memorization. In a study of the transfer of practice in memorization, H. Woodrow taught the "rules" listed below to a group of students who practiced using them in memorizing poetry and nonsense syllables. They were:

1. Learning by wholes.
2. Use of active self-testing.
3. Use of rhythm and grouping.
4. Attention to meaning and the advantage of picturing, or, depending upon the individual—otherwise symbolizing the meaning.
5. Mental alertness and concentration.
6. Confidence in ability to memorize.
7. Use of secondary associations.

Of this list only the third applies only to memorizing. Rules 2, 4, 5, and 6 apply to most learning, and all of them have repeatedly been found to improve rote learning. Woodrow compared the improvement after six hours of this training with that of a group who practiced memorizing without instruction and with a third group who took only the tests given before and after the training period. The effectiveness of the training is shown by the data in Table 11.

TABLE 11

Percentage of Gain or Loss
from Initial to Final Performance on Memory Tests

Test	Group		
	Control [a]	Practice [a]	Training [b]
Rote poetry	−33	−29	−11
Rote prose	+29	+26	+51
Facts (substance)	−5	−5	+13
Dates	+29	+38	+88
Vocabulary (Turkish-English)	−1	+3	+55
Memory span (auditory, for consonants)	+7	−6	+20

Adapted from H. Woodrow. The effect of type of training upon transference. *J. educ. Psychol.,* 1927, 18, 159–172.

[a] Control group significantly better than practice group on span. No other differences between the control and practice groups are reliable.

[b] Training group is significantly better than both control and practice groups on all tests.

Several of these "rules" are devices for making material more meaningful. Consider the sequence of numbers 6, 8, 3, 1, 3, 4, 7, 3, 8, 6. To memorize this sequence more easily you might group them in pairs as 68, 31, 34, 73, and 86 and perhaps also note that the middle pair is half the first, the last pair is the reverse of the first and, if you want to get fancy, the second pair plus the reverse of the fourth equals the first; or possibly 1347 is a familiar street address so that the arrangement 683, 1347, 386 would be easy to recall, since you only need the first number, the address, and the awareness that the last is the reverse of the first. Saying the groups rhythmically might help, too. In either procedure the number of units is reduced, and rhythm, pattern, and internal and external associations are added making a more meaningful structure. The last of the two arrangements makes the 1347 a meaningful whole, indicating that the rule about "learning by wholes" might be modified to say: Use the largest and most meaningful units you can manage, but size of unit should bow to meaning and relationships among units.

The basic principle in learning of this sort is repetition, especially of self-testing trials. Practice may continue beyond the point where apparent mastery has been achieved with profit for retention. Such practice is called overlearning; even complete nonsense may be remembered indefinitely if sufficiently overlearned. Remember *hic, haec, hoc, huius, huius, huius,* or " 'Twas brillig and the slithy toves did gyre and gimbel in the wabe," or $\therefore \triangle ABC \cong \triangle A'B'C'$ by SAS? The effect of overlearning may be described as permitting the integration of several discrete responses into unitary response sequences, as in these examples.

These principles need to be modified with more complex and potentially meaningful materials. Sheer repetition can in time reduce meaning to the

Schools, Teachers, and Subjects

Do these problems:	Given the following empty jars as measures			Obtain the required amount of water
	A	B	C	
1	29	3	—	20
2	21	127	3	100
3	14	163	25	99
4	18	43	10	5
5	9	42	6	21
6	20	59	4	31
7	23	49	3	20
8	15	39	3	18
9	28	76	3	25
10	18	48	4	22
11	14	36	8	6

Percentage Solving Problems 7 and 8 and 10 and 11 by Group and Solution Type (See Caption)

Problems	Control		Experimental			
			Plain		DBB	
	E-Solutions	D-Solutions	E-Solutions	D-Solutions	E-Solutions	D-Solutions
7 and 8	0	100	81	19	55	45
10 and 11	0	100	64	36	30	70

Figure 6. In the problems above, the task is to obtain exactly the required amount of water using only the given jars—A, B, and C—which hold exactly the amounts specified. Before reading further do the water jar problems above. Experimental subjects were given the problems in the order above and after a chance to try were shown the solutions to problems 1 (A − 3B) and 2 (B − A − 2C). They then were left to work out the remaining solutions (plain group). Another experimental group (DBB) was also told to write "Don't be blind" on their papers after problem 6. A control group did problems 1, 7, 8, 9, 10, 11 only. The Einstellung (habituation or set) effect is shown by the large percentages of E-solutions (B − A − 2C) in contrast to D-solutions (A + C and A − C) among subjects given problems 2-6. Elementary, secondary, college, and adult groups all showed this effect. The data above are for college students. (Adapted from A. S. Luchins. Mechanization in problem solving: the effect of Einstellung. Psychol. Monog., 1942, 54, Whole #248.)

detriment of transfer by making the responses more automatic and less flexible. This mechanization can be particularly harmful in problem-solving situations if the habituated response is a solution pattern rather than a part which fits all such problems. For example, solving the problems in Figure 6 is not hindered by mechanical addition and subtraction skills but it is by "blind" solution techniques. Thus, even the modified rule about "learning by wholes" becomes suspect in problem-solving contexts. The rule about self-testing also becomes less important when understanding rather than recall is the goal, perhaps because understanding improves recall.

In sum, the "rules" for memorizing (aside from the ones about concentration and confidence) either add meaning to material or must be modified as meaning becomes important. It follows that, although the nature of the material being learned is not an important influence on learning processes if meaning is excluded, this exclusion is difficult to achieve.

Meaning

Meaning in its simplest
form is a function of association. Even the so-called nonsense syllables—for example, ZUJ, TIB, DIF—differ in meaningfulness (ZUJ least, DIF most) though none of the three is a word. The frequency with which such syllables appear in words is closely related to their meaningfulness. This frequency is an important variable in learning nonsense syllable lists; frequent and varied experience with any materials enhances their meaning greatly.

If a student has had little experience with something he is asked to study it may be largely meaningless to him. If study does not rectify this, whatever learning occurs may be largely by rote. But since efforts to memorize usually involve getting some sort of meaning, the student lacking an appropriate background may grasp at any straw or association he can find—as did the student who defined "syntax" as "the money you put in the collection plate." When no meaning is available to the student he has no way of judging the adequacy of his response.

Simple associations are not all there is to meaning. A young child may have many associations with the word "eight"— it is the age of his brother; it is part of the street address of a neighbor; it comes after the word seven when one is "counting to ten" for a game or to please an adult, and so on—yet he does not grasp the concept of eightness. The word has meaning for him but these meanings may not include the ideas of one more than seven, a collection of a certain size, or any of the other cardinal or ordinal aspects of the number. Above all, he may not understand its place in the number system, its distinction as a real number, as a rational number, or as a positive integer, and its relation to other numbers in those sets (see Figure 7).

As this example implies, some meanings result from chance associations in daily life; they may or may not be numerous and they may or may not be accompanied by strong feelings and emotion. Other meanings belong to the structural categories of the subject into which the material fits (positive integers), which then carry with them the meanings from the relationships among these categories (subset of the rational numbers). Finally, some meanings are derived from the relationships among the elements in the category to which the material is assigned ($2 \times 4 = 8$). The two kinds of meaning, associative and structural, are both products of learning, and the amount and kind of meaning something has for a person indicates what and how much he has learned about it.

Since meaning facilitates retention and transfer, the more meaning one can bring to a learning task the more efficiently the new learning will proceed. Again it follows that readiness, intelligence, and achievement measures are all ways of assessing how much meaning a person can bring to a learning situation. Viewed this way, meaning appears to be a word used to describe prior learning that helps further learning. However, this is too simple. The

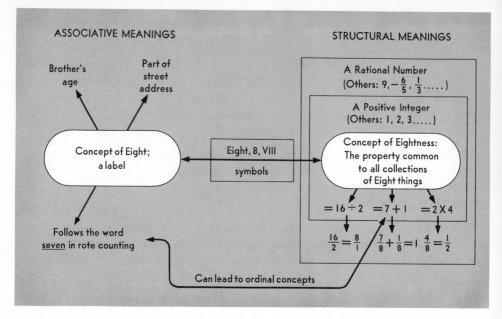

ASSOCIATIVE MEANINGS   STRUCTURAL MEANINGS

Figure 7. Some meaning of "eight." The associative meanings, unlike the structural meanings which involve relationships among concepts, are usually independent of one another and cannot be "discovered" logically. The structural meanings may be learned by rote, in which case they may have only associative meanings.

facilitating effect depends on what kind of organization and structure has been imposed on the material. In the Luchins study (Figure 6), the structure of the first few problems was often imposed on the later ones, which then led to negative, not positive, transfer effects. Evidently any old structure won't do; some have more relevance and more flexibility than others.

One way of describing the standard school subjects is to say that they are structures, developed by man over time, that he has found to be particularly relevant and flexible ways of dealing with various aspects of experience —that is, they are ways of assigning meaning to experience that tend to maximize positive transfer. This assertion applies most clearly to the end product of learning a school subject; in the early stages of learning the ability to make use of what has been already learned may be almost nil. In some subjects it may not be until after he has done graduate work that a student begins to see how broad the potential meaning of his subject may be. However, in most cases some meaning accompanies learning from the beginning, and there is usually a perceptible ability to use the learning for both further learning in the subject itself and in thinking and problem-solving. Usually this ability grows as learning proceeds. So, since a major difference between high and low intelligence is the ability to use learning, school learning and the development of intelligence would seem to be pretty much the same thing. Yet somehow a high school diploma, a college degree, or a graduate degree does not guarantee brilliance or even common sense. A closer look at what sort of learning a school subject can involve will help explain the discrepancy. The subjects of reading and history will be used as examples.

Two School Subjects

Reading involves several kinds of responses and psychological processes. Reading specialists talk about discrimination learning, perceptual learning, rote learning, learning to think, critical thinking, and problem-solving; all these are aspects of the reading process and are involved in learning to read. Reading also calls for motor activity—the eye movements of reading—and these motor skills have much to do with differences found among people in their reading. By means of a device called an eyemovement camera, it has been found that the eyes of a good reader, in contrast to those of a poor reader, move in a more orderly way along a line of print with fewer left to right movements or regressions; his fixations (pauses to look—words are seen between movements, not during movement) are usually fewer and more evenly spaced.

The development of these motor skills is a part of learning to read as are the related skills of visual discrimination. When some "phonics" are included in reading instruction, as is almost always the case, auditory discrimination is involved. In any case a good deal of rote memorization is necessary; the names and sounds of letters and letter combinations, the names and functions of punctuation marks, and the like are practiced extensively and usually substantially overlearned. The number of generalizations is rather small. One is that certain letters grouped together make a symbol for a word, and this symbol uniquely represents the word (unlike a pictorial symbol of, say, a table, which may represent table, furniture, or a use for wood). It would be stretching things a bit to talk about the principles or higher-order concepts of reading as a subject in itself. Although learning these skills and concepts is a part of learning to read, neither separately nor in combination can they be said adequately to define or describe reading or learning to read.

It is commonly said that reading is a process of acquiring (or deriving) meaning from written material. The facts, concepts, and skills just mentioned are usually held to be necessary but not sufficient for adequate reading. Texts on reading instruction are replete with illustrations of children who have some or all of these skills so that they can say the words they see written, but who "cannot read," that is, cannot get meaning from the material. We need not argue whether or not "saying words" can be called reading, since all will agree that understanding is the appropriate goal of reading and that all other goals are subsidiary, their importance depending on their contribution to this major goal. Reading, then, involves a hierarchy of learning, starting with bits of information leading to specific and then more general concepts, and developing from limited and specific skills to more and more general skills—all of which put together, through the processes involved in understanding the material, can be called reading ability. In reading, understanding refers not to the subject of reading but to the content of the material being read. It has been demonstrated repeatedly that reading ability varies from subject to subject. Progress in reading requires progress in understanding the things written about.

This hierarchy of knowledge and skill, the structure of reading as a subject, does not necessarily represent the sequence of development of this ability. It seems more probable that the "higher" processes—the critical thinking, problem-solving, and emotional and æsthetic thinking that lead to understanding—are properly a part of reading almost from the very beginning. At the end of learning they are the only "visible" parts, the only parts the reader is aware of. The rest has become automated through overlearning.

The way in which the skills underlying reading are organized or structured depends at least in part on the structure of the language or other symbol system or code to be read. Since one code is usually used during initial instruction in another code, relationships among them are clearly important.* Written language is closely related to spoken language and both are used in teaching reading. Learning to write usually accompanies learning to read, but how these two tasks influence each other is not well established. It is reasonable to assume that problems in one lead to problems in the other and that generally there is some positive transfer between reading and writing. However, that they are at least somewhat distinct abilities is demonstrated by the examples of adult aphasics whose brain damage has disrupted one language ability but not another (speaking but not writing, writing but not reading, and so on).

In sum, reading is a process of getting meaning that has a psychological structure represented by a hierarchy of skills and concepts. This hierarchy is determined by the structure of the language and the symbol system used to represent the language. For most people ability to read is limited by (a) their facility with language, (b) the adequacy of their reading skills as such, and (c) by their limitations in the content area of the material.

Since reading is a somewhat different kind of school subject from most others (some call it a "tool" subject in contrast to a "content" subject), a look at one of the standard academic subjects, or "disciplines," is in order.

Any of the academic subjects have three general characteristics worth discussing here. History will serve as an example. History is, first, a set of facts, concepts, and generalizations; but it is more than a body of knowledge; it is, second, a way of thinking about past and present events, a way of understanding a class of events (that is, historical events); and finally it is a way of finding out about these events, a way of interpreting, organizing, and evaluating them.

The supply of historical facts is boundless. By themselves they are pretty meaningless. Stating them is analogous at times to the "word-saying" in reading referred to before. Any child can learn to say "The Russo-Japanese War in 1904–5 changed the balance of power in Asia." But what does this mean to him? Before understanding this, a child would have to know a number of concepts about time, distance, nations, governments, war, and so forth, from which the somewhat more special and abstract concept of "balance of power" could be developed. Putting facts and concepts into some order or

* The first code a person learns, that is, his native spoken language, is a fundamental factor in most further learning, for this learning passes through or is mediated by this code and thus shaped and structured by it. It is probably rare that language does not shape thought. How many people learn to think in purely mathematical symbols? (See in this series J. B. Carroll. *Language and thought.* Englewood Cliffs, N. J.: Prentice-Hall, 1964.)

structure is the business of both historians and history students, and the purpose is to get meaning. Such arrangements can lead to generalizations that further enhance meaning. Some generalizations require a substantial background before they make much sense; others do not. That the way people live, as represented by their food, clothing, and shelter, has changed over time can be easily illustrated for, and understood by, many children in the primary grades; in contrast, a radical-to-conservative pendulum theory, or cyclical theory, of political history may pose problems of comprehension for high school students.

The concepts of food, clothing, and shelter involved in the first of these generalizations are relatively concrete compared to the notions of radical and conservative used in the second. The more abstract a concept the more structural meaning in contrast to associative meaning it is likely to have. A full understanding of history would involve the development of an elaborate structure of many concepts of varying abstractness whose relationships to each other make the framework on which much of its meaning depends.

One of the nicer things about history is that one man's structure is sometimes another's nonsense. For example, some historians claim that the North won the Civil War just because it won a military victory, and around this notion they build a structure of Reconstruction and post-Reconstruction American history. Theoretically, a theory or structure must fit the facts, but often, it turns out, facts are either altered ("reinterpreted") to fit the theory or ignored. Thus a more inclusive view of the Civil War, which makes a distinction between military and ultimate victory, holds that the South is currently winning by means of its control of national policy through the chairmanships of congressional committees. The development of an adequate structure by an individual requires the development of the skills and abilities that characterize a competent historian. The "historian" who lacks these abilities will often create structures that merit the label nonsense in the manner just illustrated.

The more general abilities involved in organizing and interpreting historical data have not been studied by psychologists, but presumably some of the underlying basic skills are those necessary to reading the symbol systems or codes a student of history must face. Although written languages are major avenues for learning history, there are other codes of importance such as recordings, pictures, charts, graphs, and maps.

Thus, history involves a hierarchy of things to be learned, starting with bits of information leading to specific, then more general concepts, and developing from limited to more general skills; all of which put together through the processes involved in getting meaning can become a fairly general ability to develop and deal with historical materials. As in reading, there is no reason to claim that this hierarchy represents the proper sequence of learning.

Reading and history are quite different school subjects in many ways, but, like all school subjects, they have a structure whose relationship to the meanings their study can offer to students is fundamental. History can have meaning in itself; it has a specific content with an elaborate (if controversial) structure. In contrast, the content structure of reading can be forgotten by all but reading teachers. But both subjects are concerned with ways of learning or developing understanding. Reading is normally learned so thoroughly and practiced so much that transfer is almost no problem. History as a process of understanding is rarely learned as well, partly because the content is restricted to certain categories that involve some particularly difficult and abstract concepts (for example, time concepts, democracy, and the like), partly because the process is less well defined and understood (if you think reading experts argue, you should hear some historians), and partly because the modes of presentation and communication are more varied.

Knowledge and Ability

The largely theoretical discussion in the preceding pages is intended to explain why in discussions of school learning it is convenient to distinguish between learning the conceptual structure of a subject—acquiring a knowledge and understanding of its principles and meaning—and learning to use this knowledge in thinking and further learning—developing an ability. These two categories are crudely related to the five intellectual operations postulated by Guilford and presented in Table 2 (p. 13). Knowledge as used here consists largely of cognition but includes memory as well; rote learning involves a particularly limited portion of the abilities being used and developed during the acquisition of knowledge. Thus, the word ability will be used only when the operations involve substantial use of productive thinking (convergent and divergent) or evaluation. Information concerning the abilities involved in school subjects is too scant for Guilford's more adequate scheme to be used readily.

The degree to which these two kinds of learning can proceed independently of each other is indicated in several studies. In one case, M. M. Kostick, who was comparing high school boys and girls, used a measure of factual information, one of knowledge of principles, and one of ability to apply the principles to obtain the solutions of problems. The subject matter materials used were science and home economics. He found that in the latter subject the boys knew fewer facts and fewer principles but solved more problems than the girls. In science they stood higher on all three measures. His conclusion that boys are more intelligent than girls ignores the possibility or probability that problem-solving was stressed in the science materials the boys had studied and not in the home economics material the girls had studied. Certainly women have no monopoly on failure to make intelligent use of knowledge.* Measures of retention of factual material, the ability to draw inferences from the facts, and the ability to apply principles derived from these facts often appear unrelated when college students are tested on materials from courses they have taken.

Generalizations can be memorized, thereby treating them as facts, and knowledge can be acquired without learning to use it. School subjects do differ in the degree to which rote learning, acquiring knowledge, and using knowledge is most prominent but both teachers and students can manipulate this prominence to some degree. Luchins, for example, reported that students from some schools found it easier to overcome the effects of mechanization than students from other schools (see Figure 6). He maintains that the less flexible students (who gave E-solutions) had teachers who emphasized cor-

* M. M. Kostick. A study of transfer: sex differences in the reasoning process. *J. educ. Psychol.*, 1954, 45, 449–458.

rect knowledge, while the more flexible students were in schools that encouraged independent development of ideas. Nevertheless, in reading, the development of a broadly useful ability is emphasized in all schools. One could learn about reading without being able to do it; this is rare. In history one can learn a great deal without developing the abilities of a historian; this is common. Perhaps schooling and the development of ability should be one and the same, but evidently they do not have to be.

Some aspects of acquiring knowledge and developing ability are considered in the next chapter. For now we can say that although the processes of learning are partly a function of the subjects being studied, differences among schools are probably more a consequence of the degree to which students are taught or encouraged to learn by rote, to understand the conceptual structure of the subjects, or to develop their various abilities. Perhaps school policies influence the emphasis put on one or another of these approaches to learning; perhaps they reflect it. We don't know. Certainly a student's prior training affects the kind of learning he tends to emphasize, and when a large proportion of a student body habitually treats a subject as, say, something to be learned only to pass tests rather than as something to think about and use, pressure is exerted on other students to do likewise and on teachers to accept the scheme. The scales measuring intellectual press in the CCI, such as Achievement, Reflectiveness, and Understanding, contain items that could probably differentiate schools according to their characteristic approach to learning.

Teachers in many subjects have considerable freedom to choose among these emphases, and although few would publicly avow a preference for rote learning, casual observation indicates that some teachers nonetheless encourage it. Perhaps differences of this sort among teachers could be included in studies of teacher effectiveness. But since the conditions under which a teacher must work, including the composition of his class, are not usually of his own choosing, he is not entirely free in this matter. If, for example, there is no laboratory and science is learned from textbooks, it seems probable that students will become more accustomed to acquiring knowledge than learning how to use it.

What a student is asked, urged, led, or made to do in school determines what he will learn and how he will change. Although modified by the individual's own personality, the psychological forces created by the school's organization, students, faculty, and curriculum determine the nature of these activities; yet research on these matters has been far less enlightening than these statements would lead one to expect. One reason is that schools at all levels tend to have characteristics which reinforce those of the student; that is, in most cases schools, taken as a whole, reflect and exemplify the populations they serve, and thus their students develop in the directions one would predict from their background. Therefore, a school may seem to have had no effect on a student because he doesn't appear to have changed. As the research on teachers exemplifies, research studies have paid too little attention to the kinds of intellectual operations students have learned to perform. This, after all, is the central area of a school's concern and presumably the part of a student's life over which it has the greatest control. More specific connections are needed between the research discussed so far and the studies of learning considered in the next chapter.

School Learning   Some years ago, B. F.

Skinner reported that if food is mechanically presented

to a hungry pigeon on some regular and frequent schedule

not connected with the bird's behavior, a "superstitious"

response will appear. This response (for example, hop-

ping or turning or bowing) may become a prominent

feature of the bird's behavior in the experimental situa-

tion. The repeated appearance of the food reinforces, or

strengthens, the response, which originally was just an

occasional natural action, in spite of the lack of causal

relation between the response and the reinforcement.*

  * B. F. Skinner. 'Superstition' in the pigeon. *J. exp. Psychol.,*
1948, 38, 168–172.

4

The three major topics to be considered in this chapter—transfer of training, the law of effect, and motivation—have long been havens for misconceptions developed in an analogous fashion. Psychologists and educators, although they might be expected to know better, are probably as guilty of perpetuating myth and superstition about school learning as anybody else, perhaps because the activities and events that accompany school learning are so numerous and varied that there are many opportunities to ascribe the learning observed to a concurrent but unrelated event.

In most cases when a series of experiences are accompanied or followed by a persistent change in behavior, learning is inferred. More specifically, when an individual engages in practice or training activities and when observations of his performance indicate the performance has changed, learning is usually assumed to have occurred. Studies of learning examine these changes in performance in relation to the practice operations and the practice conditions.

When one considers the variety of performances that can be observed, the variety of changes that can occur, and, above all, the variety of conditions surrounding practice that can exist, any apparent simplicity of this description quickly evaporates. As noted in Chapter 2, evidence for stating that learning has occurred because of some specific school activity or experience is often slender, as when teachers give examinations and infer from the scores that the students have learned. This assumption is often reasonable enough, but a teacher rarely knows what parts of the performance on the examination represent (a) learning before the course began, (b) learning from other concurrent courses and nonschool activities, and (c) learning from activity for this course. It is the purpose of scientific procedures to eliminate such difficulties. A test given before instruction begins can be used to assess prior learning, and comparisons with control groups allow for the concurrent learnings. But even if only changes in performance are considered, the transfer effects of prior learning are usually a part of the changes; therefore, to understand school learning the effects of prior experience need to be assessed. To accomplish this, groups with different prior training need to be compared, which is how transfer is studied (see pp. 4–5).

The law of effect refers to the fact that there is a class of events that, when they come immediately after a response or response sequence, can determine the course of learning, as the learning of a "superstition" illustrates. These reinforcements, rewards and punishments, or whatever you choose to call these events, are exceeded in importance for learning only by the students' actions that they follow. As a rule they can be studied only in situations specifically designed for that purpose. Under typical school conditions it is hard to observe all of the learners' activities during the period of practice (the time when the learning is assumed to have taken place). When a group of students "study" some material, the nature of their practice operations are often more guessed at than observed, which in turn makes discussions of the law of effect in school learning very speculative.

Some people have claimed that school learning is more difficult to study directly than other areas in psychology. It is unlikely that this is so. The problems in the study of human behavior are common to the whole science. In any case, difficult or not, the basic processes in learning are not hard to outline. For learning to occur, the learner must be aroused or activated. The forces that produce activity are called motives. Once he is active, what he learns depends first on what he does—that is, on his practice activities, which include his internal covert responses as well as his external overt actions—and second on the consequences of these actions.

But what determines what his actions will be? The external elements in the learning situation combine with the needs, abilities, and prior learning of the student to create an internal state we will call a *set*. Set determines what cues the student perceives as relevant and determines his strategies or ways of going about the task as he sees it. An advantage of a laboratory study of learning is the greater possibility of limiting and controlling the available cues. An advantage of a school study of learning is the greater possibility of using long sequences of learning experiences. Thus, laboratory work tends to emphasize stimuli, whereas school studies more often concern transfer.

TRANSFER OF TRAINING

The Ubiquity of Transfer Effects

For several reasons transfer effects are an omnipresent feature of school learning. First, prolonged and intensive work is usually necessary before there is much evidence of substantial progress towards school objectives. What students learn in any given day, week, or month is often too little to be reliably detected in an individual case, or even in a whole class. One can easily detect the temporary acquisition of particular responses within short periods of time, but teachers realized long ago that a student who writes correctly all the French words in the vocabulary test at the end of the week may not appear to know them a few weeks later when he attempts a translation that includes these words. A seventh grade class spends a month writing and correcting ten-minute themes; yet the quality of the writing in their answers to brief essay questions on a history test is apparently unchanged by this experience. To be sure, some of the students do better the second time, but others do less well. The themes themselves may well show improvement but progress in general writing ability is slow, a fact that most teachers at any level would concede even though some prefer to talk about the incompetence of the student's earlier teachers.

Thus, schools are usually concerned with the development of rather broad general abilities—the ability to read a wide variety of materials rapidly and with understanding, the ability to write well, the ability to use mathematics in many different situations intelligently and efficiently, the ability to see a public event in its historical perspective, and so forth. The organization or synthesis of acquired responses and limited skills into large general abilities is a central concern of educational psychology. If for no other reasons than practical ones, the study of learning at this broad, general level often can be conducted in schools far better than any other place. The typical high school graduate has probably spent well over ten thousand hours in the classroom. To get people to spend even a hundred hours in a laboratory is exceedingly difficult.

Lastly, school learning usually begins in the middle. Ordinarily students have had a long history of prior experience relevant in some degree to the immediate task, and a student's readiness to learn something is affected by the knowledge and abilities already developed. Most children, in most subjects, most of the time, are being asked to learn material about which they have already learned a good deal. In long division, the student uses his already developed ability to read numbers and mathematical symbols, to write them, to add, subtract, multiply, and divide. Thus, a study of learning long division is in large measure a study of transfer. It is the study of how partially developed abilities are further developed and how a number of abilities of limited scope are organized or synthesized into larger, broader abilities. This is one reason why educational psychologists have devoted so much attention to individual differences in students' abilities. This is also one of the reasons why transfer of training is the central topic in any discussion of school learning.

Several of the earliest experimental studies of transfer quickly became standard references for educators and educational psychologists even though some of the most frequently cited did not really deal with school learning. Thorndike and Woodworth's studies of transfer in estimating the size of pieces of paper of various shapes, James' study of memorizing, and Judd's report on dart throwing, all of them published more than 50 years ago, are prominent examples. Much of the early experimental work in school learning dealt with transfer, and it became one of the few major topics in the psychology of learning where theories derived from research have played a prominent role in educational doctrine. Attention was initially directed towards proving the falsity of the theory of faculty psychology and its doctrine of mental discipline.

Formal Discipline

The notion that the mind,
or soul, or intellect, has a number of more or less independent components has been popular among psychologists and philosophers for centuries. One version of this view, influential among philosophers in the eighteenth century, among educators during the nineteenth century, and among newspaper editors in the twentieth century, called these components mental faculties. These faculties were such things as memory, will, attention, sympathy, and so forth. The theory of formal discipline held that a faculty could be strengthened by exercise in a manner more or less analogous to the building of a muscle. Various school subjects in the curriculum were presumed to strengthen one or another of the faculties of the mind. Plane geometry was an exercise in reasoning, and it was assumed that studying plane geometry improved general reasoning. Schools indulged in extensive demands on their students for memory work on the grounds that practice in memorizing improved memory; the more things memorized, the better memory would become. It is still customary to refer to various subject fields as disciplines because each of the then-accepted fields had its own mental faculty or faculties to develop or "discipline."

In one of the earliest empirical checks of this idea, William James kept track of the time it took him during an eight-day period to learn 158 lines of poetry. He then practiced learning *Paradise Lost,* 20 minutes daily for 38 days, and finally learned 158 new lines from the first poem. This second 158 lines took him somewhat longer than the first. He persuaded several students to perform similar trials. Some of them improved slightly; some did not. James argued that some of the improvements came from direct practice on the initial poem and he added, "All improvement of memory consists, then, in improvement of one's habitual method of recording facts" (James, 1890, p. 667). Although this was far from a careful experiment by today's standards, Woodrow's study (see Table 11) confirmed both that sheer practice in memorizing by educated adults will not necessarily improve performance and that improvement can come from an improvement in method of memorization. Increased familiarity with materials and conditions of practice may help also. These results appear inconsistent with the claims for formal discipline.

But what is an improved method? The answer suggested in Chapter 3 is a method that helps develop a structure appropriate to the material. If a group of individuals, after memorizing lists of numbers, have improved by developing the techniques of grouping and using rhythm, this practice might help them learn lists of nonsense syllables, but it is doubtful that it would help in learning a list of facts about the Punic Wars in the unlikely event they wanted to do so. If the practice also included attention to the use of active self-testing, to ways of developing meaning and organizing the material around meanings, then transfer of this practice to learning facts about the Punic Wars is at least possible. But if the individual has already developed such techniques, further practice with them is not likely to lead to much transfer.

Essentially the same results have been obtained in studies dealing with other "faculties." Unless something new is being learned, such as some new technique, and unless the thing learned is appropriate to the transfer situation, practice will not produce much in the way of transfer. Yet new things often are learned. A student may, deliberately or incidentally, so organize and structure the material that he derives principles. He may also develop new and more effective ways of proceeding that heighten his ability to learn other materials of the same general sort.

Although these statements suggest that only minor modifications in the theory of formal discipline are needed, these modifications severely reduce its usefulness. If practice automatically strengthens a faculty, prediction of when, how much, and under what circumstances transfer will occur would depend only on specifying the degree to which the faculty enters into any given activity. Although this is hard enough and presupposes the adequacy of the categories of faculties used, determining what new learning any practice will produce and whether this learning will be seen as relevant in a transfer situation is much more difficult. Removing the automatic, inevitable feature of the theory of formal discipline has left a gap in psychological theory that to date remains unfilled. The substitutes usually cited are Judd's generalization theory of transfer and Thorndike's theory of identical elements offered originally in 1908 and 1901, respectively.

C. H. Judd's theory of
transfer by generalization was first presented along with his report of the famous study of throwing darts at targets under water. One group of boys was given an explanation of the principle of refraction whereas the second was not. Both groups then threw darts at targets under 12 inches of water. After this task was mastered the subjects were asked to throw darts at a target now under four inches of water. Since the boys were standing at an angle to the target the change in the level of water changed the amount of refraction and thus the apparent position of the target. The group that had been told the general principle adapted more rapidly to this second task than did the other group. This result has been confirmed in other studies, but as Figure 8 shows, uninstructed groups also do better the second time. Perhaps some of these individuals generalized their experience, in effect saying to themselves, "If the target seemed displaced in this direction before, it probably is again." They wouldn't know that it was displaced less, but this generalization about the two situations would help and would be better than sheer trial and error. Conceivably this group could even derive the principle of refraction for themselves with enough experience at a variety of depths and angles.

The preceding paragraph has referred to three somewhat different meanings of the term "generalization"—the principle itself, the process of extending it to cover a new situation, and the process of deriving the principle from experience. To say that a principle applies to more than a single situation is merely to say that it is a somewhat general principle, not a single fact. Derivation of a principle is usually described as involving the processes of concept formation and attainment which include not only generalization but abstraction and discrimination as well. Taking a known principle and extending it to cover new situations is the process of generalization Judd emphasized and deemed the essence of transfer. Learning a principle, whether with or without instruction, was a prerequisite for transfer in Judd's view, and he felt that the organized principles represented by an academic subject are the broadest, most abstract, and hence potentially the most easily generalized of ideas. He nevertheless emphasized the need for specific concrete experience. Thus, shooting at one water level was necessary before the experimental group could do better than the group without knowledge of the principle.

Identical Elements

To refute the theory of
of formal discipline E. L. Thorndike and R. S. Woodworth examined the effect of training on the ability to judge the size of pieces of paper of various shapes. They found that practice in judging the size of a set of rectangles led to the most improvement on these materials and to greater facility with another set of rectangles than with a set of nonrectangular shapes. Presumably, sheer familiarity with elements of rectangles promoted better discrimination of relevant differences, but probably the subjects also developed methods of learning to judge size more appropriate for rectangles than for

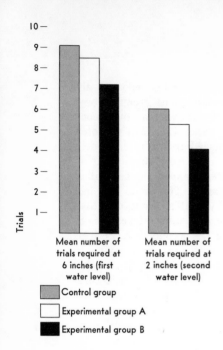
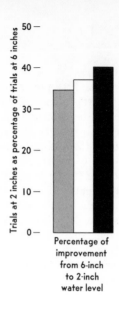

Figure 8. Effect of instruction about the principle of refraction on target shooting. Only the experimental groups were told about refraction. Group B was told further how water-level changes shift the image. The differences at 6 inches are not significant (P > .10) but those at the 2 inch level are (P < .05). (Adapted from G. Hendrickson and W. H. Schroeder. Transfer of training in learning to hit a submerged target. J. educ. Psychol., 1941, 32, 205–213.)

other shapes. They also found that practice in spotting verbs quickly on a page did not help in finding prepositions at all. They concluded, "Improvement in any single mental function need not improve the ability in functions commonly called by the same name. . . . Spread of practice occurs only where identical elements are covered in the influencing and influenced functions." Thorndike wrote later, "These experiments show very clearly the influence of: The acquisition during special training, (1) of ideas of method and habits of procedure and also (2) a facility with certain elements that appeared in many other complexes." (Thorndike, 1913 Vol. II, p. 398.) This is Thorndike's theory of identical elements. These identical elements may be in the learning materials and situations or in the learning strategies.

Thorndike's theory, although it has often been interpreted to mean that training must be specific and that broad transfer is not to be expected, provides a major clue about how transfer may be increased. A device that increases the number of identical elements in the training and transfer situations will tend to increase transfer effects. Many experimental investigations of school learning have confirmed this inference and the procedure has come to be called "teaching for transfer." For example, the traditional high school course in plane geometry typically produces little improvement on measures of reasoning or of ability to solve algebraic problems, even among students who understand rather than memorize theorems. But a number of reports indicate that this situation is partly remedied when serious attempts are made to teach for transfer, that is, when patterns of thought and applications to nongeometric situations are emphasized.

In his discussions of school work, Thorndike made much of the importance of study procedures. Most educators today still consider methods of study a source of possible general academic improvement for most students. Instances of negative rather than positive effects are often found in this area. The student who habitually skims for the general idea in his reading is bewildered when he tries this technique in a mathematics text. Similarly the individual who reads each sentence painstakingly, analyzing it carefully as might be appropriate in reading mathematics, fails to understand how anybody can get through all the reading assigned in a literature course. Teaching for transfer in this context would involve helping the student make appropriate distinctions, helping him discriminate between similar and seemingly similar situations.

The merits of the theory of identical elements are also the sources of its weaknesses. The elements that may be identical in two situations are ways of proceeding or methods, information or knowledge, stimuli, apparently anything. Also, nothing in the theory permits direct prediction of when an individual will perceive the identity and when he will not. Lastly, the theory does not specify the manner in which transfer occurs. The theory of formal discipline dealt with these questions as far as general patterns of behavior and abilities were concerned and Judd attempted the same thing for knowledge. Since the acquisition of knowledge and the development of ability can occur separately, transfer of these two sorts of learning may be considered separately.

Transfer of Abilities

The theory of formal discipline overstated and inadequately described the otherwise reasonable, verifiable proposition that extended practice often leads to improved ability to perform in a general area. The difficulties with this theory were the expectations of automatic, general improvement from any practice, and the set of abilities used. The somewhat overzealous rejection of formal discipline among educators and psychologists eager to be scientific in the early part of the century (there is nothing like hindsight) meant that the transfer involved in developing general abilities was inadequately studied for many years. It was held instead that since transfer must be limited to areas with many identical elements there is essentially no such thing as a general ability, only specific skills; therefore the task of educational psychology was to list the specific skills schools should teach. Curiously, at this same time tests of general ability came into widespread use in the schools. The role of ability in learning was discussed in Chapter 2, where it was pointed out that differences in the use of prior learning are the central feature of differences in ability. Although such transfer is no more inevitable than any other kind, some amount is the rule, which is why individuals who do not use their abilities as well as others do, rate the label underachiever.

The development of abilities was long treated as a topic separate from transfer of training, even by those working in both areas. This failure to transfer ideas about transfer on the part of psychologists during the first half of the century may have come partly from the uncertainty about the role of learning in children's growing abilities. The increase in ability from infancy to adulthood was obvious and was the fact on which ability tests were built. But while general background and education were known to influence intelligence, the extent of the influence remained a matter of controversy (see Chapter 6). Furthermore, convincing demonstrations of the development of ability through practice were lacking.

Several developments since World War II have changed this picture. One was the work of H. F. Harlow on what he called the formation of learning sets. Harlow worked mostly with monkeys, but he obtained similar results with preschool children. The task was to choose between two different objects; each correct choice was rewarded. There were 344 of these object-discrimination problems; in each the monkey had to learn to select the correct object. The pairs of objects changed from problem to problem. On each of the first 32 problems the subject had 50 trials; thereafter only six trials per problem were given. Average learning curves for trials 1–6 are shown in Figure 9. In the first problems the course of learning was typical of most descriptions of learning, showing gradual increases in accuracy. After 25 problems, the improvement, particularly on trial 2, indicated considerable transfer; after several hundred problems the improvement was remarkable. By this time most subjects were responding correctly on trial 2; that is, they were learning immediately. One might describe this behavior as insightful. Children ranging in age from two to five years learned more rapidly than the monkeys (the children were above average in intelligence), but the results were otherwise identical.

Figure. 9. Discrimination learning curves for successive blocks of problems. The percentage of correct responses on trial 1 is at chance necessarily. The points plotted are averages for the whole group for the set of problems indicated. (From H. F. Harlow. The formation of learning sets. Psychol. Rev., 1949, 56, 51–65.)

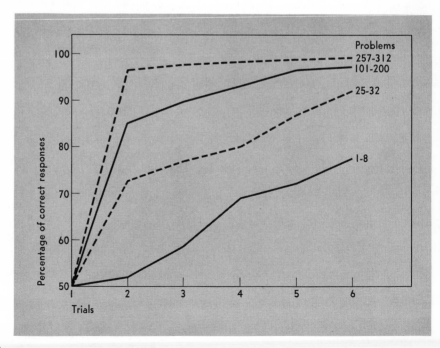

Later the original group of monkeys was given a series of discrimination-reversal problems; in these, after seven, nine, or eleven trials the "correct" or rewarded object was changed for the remaining eight trials. The object that was correct at first became incorrect, and vice versa. A set of curves similar to those shown in Figure 9 was obtained, but the rate of improvement was more rapid. By the time the monkeys had had about 50 of these discrimination-reversal problems they could respond correctly on the second reversal trial. Having discovered on the first reversal trial that the previously rewarded response was no longer correct, they learned to reverse on the next trial. Thus, there was not only transfer from discrimination problem to discrimination problem and transfer from discrimination-reversal problem to discrimination-reversal problem, but also transfer from the original set of discrimination problems to the set of discrimination-reversal problems. The rate of learning to learn for the latter and presumably more difficult set of tasks was far more rapid than for the first set of direct discrimination problems.

Here, then, is an example of just the sort of phenomenon predicted by the theory of formal discipline, but the following facts need emphasis:

1. The effect of practice on a single problem was small. Extended practice on many problems was required before the learning set was fully formed. Some transfer studies have used only one problem; few transfer studies have provided as much practice with so many similar tasks.

2. Young children have not had years of experience in discrimination learning. Adults should be correct on trial 2 in very short order on this task; thus, practice could not show much effect other than gains in speed. James, Thorndike and Woodworth, and many others studied individuals with much prior practice.

3. Transfer to the reversal problem still required some direct practice, but much less. Frequently little or no practice in the transfer situation has been provided. The Luchins study of mechanization or set in problem-solving indicates that when the practiced problems are so similar that the solution patterns are the same, immediate transfer effects may be negative (see Figure 6).

Substantial transfer effects from practice will be found more often if these facts are recognized in the design of research. G. T. Buswell, after developing the thesis that the function of the school is to help the pupil learn how to learn, said:

. . . Obviously, the crucial psychological problem for such a theory is that of transfer. How can the learning attained carry over and spread to other situations as they are encountered? How can the outcomes of education be generalized so as to be broad in scope? Certainly the early types of experiments on transfer, such as Thorndike's study of the effect of practice in judging the size of circles upon ability to judge the size of squares, would contribute little. The problem could not be met by studying the carry-over of one academic subject to another subject. Rather, the studies that have significance are those that deal with transfer at the general rather than the specific level; with the development of intellectual habits that may spread widely, rather than with narrow intellectual functions. Studies such as Harlow's experiments with chimpanzees in learning how to learn have high significance for such a theory of education . . .*

To pursue this line we also need some guide for determining how broad intellectual functions may be. The discrimination learning set developed by Harlow's subjects was not a very broad ability. Adding the discrimination-reversal set, however, broadened it. It may be guessed that if practice is varied so that a number of related sets are formed, the sets become organized into hierarchical groups of both specific and general abilities. The rather widely accepted scheme proposed by Guilford (see Table 2) may be taken as an approximation of what is needed.

As a means of tying together the facts about ability development and transfer, G. A. Ferguson has proposed the following:

(1) The abilities of man, including the reasoning, number, perceptual and spatial abilities, and whatever is subsumed under intelligence, are attributes of behavior, which through learning have attained a crude stability or invariance in the adult, and, as they develop in the child, exhibit considerable stability over limited periods of time at particular age levels.

(2) Biological factors in the formation of ability are not excluded. These fix limiting conditions. The implication is that within these boundaries the range of variation in ability attributable to learning is substantial. Thus emphasis is diverted from biological to environmental determination in the formation of ability.

(3) Cultural factors prescribe what shall be learned and at what age; consequently different cultural environments lead to the development of different patterns of ability. Those abilities which are culturally valid, and correlate with numerous performances demanded by the culture, are those that show a marked increment with age.

(4) Abilities emerge through a process of differential transfer and exert their effects differentially in learning situations. Those that transfer and produce their effects at one stage of learning may differ from those at another.

(5) The concept of a general intellective factor, and the high correlations between many psychological tests, are explained by the process of positive transfer, the distinctive abilities which emerge in the adult in any culture being those that tend to facilitate rather than inhibit each other. Learning itself is viewed as a process whereby the abilities of man become differentiated, this process at any stage being facilitated by the abilities already possessed by the individual.†

Ferguson points out that as an ability reaches its limit of development in a person as determined by his nature and by the possibilities in the learning sets involved, further practice constitutes overlearning and thereafter contributes to the stability of the ability. Upon occasion an adult's ability may undergo substantial improvement because new learning sets are formed—presumably when he begins to learn in an area in which he has had little prior experience. But for any profound change he would have to be plunged into entirely new experiences so that a whole group of sets is formed. Since this rarely happens, adult abilities are fairly stable.

After the early years of high school the kinds of learning activities ex-

* G. T. Buswell. Educational theory and the psychology of learning. *J. educ. Psychol.*, 1956, 47, p. 180.

† G. A. Ferguson. On transfer and the abilities of man. *Canad. J. Psychol.*, 1956, 10, 121.

pected of students remain relatively constant. The individual may go on acquiring knowledge, but the abilities called for in its acquisition change very little. For example, reading becomes one of the major abilities in the acquisition of knowledge in school and reading abilities cease to improve at least by the end of high school and often much before that, even though most people's reading abilities are less well developed than is possible for them. Their learning sets, their procedures, are too thoroughly overlearned to be changed easily. Sharp improvement in an individual's rate of reading can be rather readily obtained with no loss in comprehension. Many colleges and commercial organizations offer courses of this sort. However, although occasional individuals keep these improvements, most people soon regress to their former rate. An improvement from a typical 250 words a minute reading rate to 500 words a minute is not too difficult for many people, but only if they continue to practice over a substantial period of time does this new rate tend to stabilize and become permanent.

Most of the basic learning sets formed in school have probably stabilized by the end of the elementary school, and their organization into patterns of abilities is pretty far along. The learning activities in the upper grades are largely verbal, and just as reading progress slows, so does progress in the other abilities involved in the acquisition of knowledge. Improvement need not and often does not cease—in some cases it may continue until the person is well over 30, but it typically slows markedly between ages 13 and 16. This does not mean there is no further learning—quite the contrary. Knowledge continues to be acquired and therefore the range of areas in which abilities *can* be used continually grows.

Transfer of Knowledge

The use of acquired knowledge is sometimes called applicational transfer. The frequent failure of this transfer to occur can be puzzling. Why do so few high school graduates, all of whom have studied civics, participate in political affairs? Why do students persist in using devious arithmetic techniques in solving problems more suited to the algebra they know? Why aren't educational psychologists known as outstanding teachers? Although ability in the given area is a factor, it is not the whole story.

L. Szekely gave a "traditional" group written material about inertia and rotation and told them their understanding of the material would be tested later. Next there was a demonstration of the slower rotation of a torsion pendulum when weights are farther from the center. A "modern" group was shown the pendulum and asked to decide what effect moving the weights away from the center would have. Few of their speculations were correct. The demonstration was given next and they then were told to read the written material to find out why the effect occurred. A few days later all subjects were given a set of problems; although they did not realize that these tasks had anything to do with the instruction about inertia and rotation, in one of them the solution depended on the principle demonstrated. The results are given in Figure 10. The modern group had read the material to solve the problem of why the demonstration worked in a way they had not expected. This approach proved useful in solving the new problem although knowledge acquired could not be reproduced precisely. The group that had studied for a test could reproduce the principle twice as frequently but could use it only a third as often as the problem-oriented group.

DESIGN OF THE STUDY

Traditional Group	Told to read material, would be tested on it	Read	Saw demon- stration		Given problem 3 weeks later
Modern Group	Shown pendulum and asked to predict	Saw demon- stration	Told to read material to explain results	Read	Given problem 3 weeks later

RESULTS

| | | Solved | Stated Principle | | |
Group	n	Problem	Solvers	Nonsolvers	Total
Traditional	20	4	2	6	8
Modern	20	13	0	4	4
Both Groups	40	17	2	10	12

Figure 10. Effect of set on using knowledge in problem solving. (Adapted from L. Szekely. Productive processes in learning and thinking. Acta Psychol., *1950, 7, 388–407.)*

I. Maltzman, E. Eisman, and L. O. Brooks repeated this study and found no difference between the groups on either a retention test or the criterion problem. However, *both* groups were told they would be tested on the reading material, thereby changing the purpose in reading of the modern group to that of the traditional group.* The comparison of these two studies suggests that if Szekely's subjects had not all been naive about physics, more in both of his groups would have solved the problem. In general this kind of transfer is enhanced by thorough initial learning as well as by teaching for transfer, which here would be instruction in the application of knowledge about mechanics to various problems. Similarly in the Hendricksen and Schroeder study (see Figure 8), experimental group B was told not only the principle of refraction as was group A, but also how it applied to a change in water level. The apparently greater transfer effect in group B was presumably a consequence of this instruction. Since the instruction did not include training in shooting, experience was still of value and the effect of the knowledge was not clearly evident until a second chance to use it appeared. More work on such practice sequences is needed.

In sum, a background of relevant concepts, inclusive and abstract enough to be fitted to new material, is helpful. These concepts serve the learner by providing a framework within which and around which new knowledge may be assimilated, understood, and remembered. They provide ready-made in-

* I. Maltzman, E. Eisman, and L. O. Brooks. Some relationships between methods of instruction, personality variables, and problem-solving behavior. *J. educ. Psychol.,* 1956, 47, 71–78.

terpretations or mediators through which the learning experiences are trans-
formed into meaningful, structured knowledge. In a series of studies D. P.
Ausubel and D. Fitzgerald have given students short written passages that
provide such concepts prior to direct study of learning materials. Their data
indicate that these passages, which they call "organizers," assist learning, but
that students with higher verbal ability can develop such concepts for themselves more readily than those of lesser ability. Therefore, an organizer is
less helpful to the more verbally talented group, although self-generated
concepts may not tie in previous knowledge as well as those developed by
experts.*

Students who have the most relevant information do better than those
with the least, although in some instances ability to use knowledge may need
to be developed, as in the target-shooting studies. Similarly, Szekely's students knew very little about relating mechanical principles to concrete problems; his "modern" method in contrast to the traditional gave them practice in this activity.

Inadequacies in either ability or knowledge may be responsible for a
failure of transfer to occur. Instruction can provide knowledge and practice
can develop ability. Sometimes a student can be given information that will
partially substitute for ability in the immediate learning situation by creat-
ing a helpful direction or set. Sometimes simply telling a student how to
proceed can accomplish the same end.

Instructional Set

Teachers' instructions to
students about how to proceed may vary in their usefulness. M. C. Wittrock
gave four groups of students a 2500-word passage on Buddhism to read with
four different kinds of directions. In one the students were to note and remember the similarities and differences between Buddhism and the religions
of the Judeo-Christian tradition. The second set of directions said to look for
similarities, while the third group was told to look for differences. A fourth
group was told to understand and remember the Buddhism passage. After
25 minutes of study a test was given. Three weeks later they were given a
retention test. On measures of both learning and retention, the set created
by the instructions to understand and remember was inferior to the others.
These instructional sets, or orientations, functioned in much the way an
organizer or an appropriate learning set functions. In contrast to the "understand and remember" direction, the other directions suggested to the students how to proceed to organize and structure the learning materials.†

But many psychologists and educators believe that both prestructuring
and telling can be carried too far. The belief that self-directed learning is
better than being told is appealing. Discovering principles and working out
problem-solving procedures for oneself is said to either increase motivation
or produce more transferable sets than following someone else's directions.
Although Judd's report appears to contradict this, Szekely's appears to sup-

* D. P. Ausubel and D. Fitzgerald. Organizer, general background, and antecedent
learning variables in sequential verbal learning. *J. educ. Psychol.*, 1962, 53, 243–249.

† M. C. Wittrock. Effect of certain sets upon complex verbal learning. *J. educ.
Psychol.*, 1963, 54, 85–88.

port it. In general, studies comparing "telling" or "direction" with "discovery" procedures have produced rather inconsistent results. One reason may be the confusion about how much direction or telling has been used in the various studies. In no case can it be said that the learners were entirely undirected, since at the very least the materials with which they were to work were specified. And in most cases a considerable amount of guidance was given to the "discovery" groups. A discovery procedure often provides a means of forming or practicing learning sets. If the practice is too narrow or inadequate in amount, teacher direction may be more efficient. But it is not known just what sorts of things are more profitably told to students and what are better left for them to work out for themselves.

Obviously learning and performance are aided when attention is focused on the essential and relevant features of a situation. Teachers' instructions can assist with this, so can practice which produces appropriate learning sets, and so can knowledge of relevant principles and generalizations. These are the kinds of things involved in teaching for transfer even though the "identical elements" may be labelled in some other way. Another sort of identical element that produces transfer is an attitude.

Attitudes

Attitudes are relatively permanent tendencies to respond in consistent ways to particular classes of objects or events. They therefore create relatively stable sets. The relation between knowledge and attitudes has been treated in many ways. One of the more intriguing approaches is Festinger's theory of cognitive dissonance (Festinger, 1957). Essentially, Festinger maintains that an individual prefers to have his attitudes consistent with one another, with his knowledge, and with his actions. Inconsistencies create dissonance, and to reduce it he may modify one or both of the dissonant elements. This apparently simple idea can be used to interpret the data on attitude change.

For example, R. N. Bostrom and his colleagues * had college students answer questionnaires concerning their views on legalized gambling and on socialized medicine. Six weeks later they were assigned an essay in which each had to defend the position contrary to the more extreme attitude of the two he had earlier expressed. Later the papers were returned with one third assigned no grade, one third an A, and one third a D. The grades were assigned on a random basis. The attitude scales were immediately given again. Regardless of grade, mean change on the topic written about was greater than on the other topic. The act of constructing a defense of an attitude they opposed may have created dissonance by forcing attention upon information previously ignored, discounted, and not acknowledged as relevant. Since here these standard ways of avoiding dissonance could not be used readily, attitudes changed. As Figure 11 indicates those given an A on their work shifted more than the other two groups. This effect can be attributed to the greater shift needed when the teacher has indicated the arguments presented are acceptable than when the arguments are ignored or rejected by being marked D. These interpretations suggest that maximum attitude change will occur when

* R. N. Bostrom, J. W. Vlandis, and M. E. Rosenbaum. Grades as reinforcing contingencies and attitude change. *J. educ. Psychol.*, 1961, 52, 112–115.

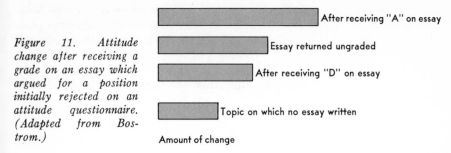

Figure 11. Attitude change after receiving a grade on an essay which argued for a position initially rejected on an attitude questionnaire. (Adapted from Bostrom.)

dissonance is greatest, provided it is not simpler to avoid conflict by not listening, selective forgetting, or the like. In other cases, changes in views may occur more readily when the amount of shift needed to produce consonance is small, since it may then be the easiest course of action. In either case, change may create other dissonances—for example, disagreement with parents—and may therefore be short lived.

From this, one can readily see why the roles played by knowledge and instruction in the modification of attitude can be large, albeit difficult to foresee, and why deliberate attempts to alter people's conceptions of race and other emotionally charged views require considerable ingenuity. But when successful, this learning transfers with particular ease.

THE LAW OF EFFECT

For some theorists, Festinger's approach is just another way of describing how the law of effect functions in learning. The law of effect as stated by Thorndike is:

To the situation, "a modifiable connection being made by him between an S and an R and being accompanied or followed by a satisfying state of affairs" man responds, other things being equal, by an increase in the strength of that connection. To a connection similar, save that an *annoying* state of affairs goes with or follows it, man responds, other things being equal, by a decrease in the strength of the connection.

The laws of connection forming or association or habit furnish education with two obvious general rules:—(1) Put together what should go together and keep apart what should not go together. (2) Reward desirable connections and make undesirable connections produce discomfort. Or, in combined form: Exercise and reward desirable connections; prevent or punish undesirable connections.*

Thorndike added that it wouldn't be necessary to say these obvious things if it weren't that they were widely misunderstood, neglected, and overlooked in both educational theory and school practice. By 1930 Thorndike had decided that the last half of his law of effect was not true. That is, he decided

---

* E. L. Thorndike. *Educational psychology*. New York: Teachers College, Columbia University, 1913, Vol. I, p. 172, and Vol. II, p. 20.

that annoying states of affairs or punishments do not weaken connections. Although psychologists are still free with their criticism of educational practice, they themselves have frequently come under attack by those who still consider the full law of effect a statement of the obvious. But as Thorndike's change of heart may suggest, the matter is not at all obvious when subjected to close analysis. Thorndike admitted from the beginning that determining what constitutes a "satisfier" or reward was not always simple.

Reinforcement

Consider again the Bostrom study cited above. The authors did not discuss either dissonance and consonance, or reward and punishment, but described the results as giving ". . . support for the hypothesis that a 'good' grade serves to reinforce the behavior for which it is administered." Of course, it can also be assumed that just as the A grades acted as rewards, the D's acted as punishments. The function of a grade can also be interpreted as giving the student information about the adequacy of his work. Although some people prefer to consider such information as a particular class of reinforcer, others prefer to speak of knowledge of results. However, all of these interpretations—and these are not the only ones—assume that the students perceived a connection between the quality of their work and the grade received. That there was no contingent relation merely illustrates that school marks may lead to behavior analogous to that of Skinner's "superstitious" pigeons. This relationship between behavior and its "consequence" is one of the most important topics in psychology, if only because reinforcement is one of the strongest and most immediately visible influences on the course of learning.

Different interpretations of the law of effect are the rule in psychology. An idea of some of these arguments may be seen in the following two statements. The first is from Skinner's well-known article proposing that schools adopt teaching machines in order to control reinforcement.

Recent improvements in the conditions which control behavior in the field of learning are of two principle sorts. The Law of Effect has been taken seriously; we have made sure that effects *do* occur and that they occur under conditions which are optimal for producing the changes called learning. Once we have arranged the particular type of consequence called a reinforcement, our techniques permit us to shape up the behavior of an organism almost at will. It has become a routine exercise to demonstrate this in classes in elementary psychology by conditioning such an organism as a pigeon. Simply by presenting food to a hungry pigeon at the right time, it is possible to shape up three or four well-defined responses in a single demonstration period—such responses as turning around, pacing the floor in the pattern of a figure-8, standing still in a corner of the demonstration apparatus, stretching the neck, or stamping the foot. Extremely complex performances may be reached through successive stages in the shaping process, the contingencies of reinforcement being changed progressively in the direction of the required behavior. The results are often quite dramatic. In such a demonstration one can *see* learning take place. A significant change in behavior is often obvious as the result of the single reinforcement.

A second important advance in technique permits us to maintain behavior in given states of strength for long periods of time. Reinforcements continue to be important, of course, long after an organism has learned *how* to do something, long after it has acquired behavior. They are necessary to maintain the behavior in strength.*

W. C. H. Prentice, however, seriously questions our understanding of those things that Skinner asserts we have just come to understand.

The admirable parsimony of behavior theories like Hull's or the learning theory of Thorndike to which it owes so much, has led several generations of academic theorists to persist in the attempt to deal with motivation without reference to cognition as such. We have, in fact, continued to hope that we could do away with motivational problems by explaining all behavior in terms of instigation by stimuli, merely noting that the conditions of instigation include the prior influence of what we call positive and negative reinforcement on the formation of habits. But the system has not worked. The motivational problems will not go away. . . .
. . . We must take as a fact of nature the finding that, in man at least, genuine and permanent "reinforcers" may be acquired during the individual's lifetime. Some adult motives do seem to have all the characteristics of bodily needs despite having obviously been acquired through some kind of training or experience. The grave difficulty is that we know nothing about the conditions of such training, if indeed the training is to be held responsible. Some acts long performed in the service of a basic satisfaction ultimately seem to become self-sustaining; others do not. Which are the differences among them? Does the difference really lie, as is so often proposed, in the nature of the reinforcement or in its frequency? Or should we not ask whether it lies in the nature of the acts themselves? †

The basic argument concerns what things may be called reinforcers and why they function as they do. The advantage of the term reinforcement over reward illustrates one aspect of the problem. It often appears that certain things act as reinforcers which do not fit our everyday understanding of the word reward. For example, a clearly unpleasant electric shock for each correct response can lead to efficient learning. Is this reinforcer a reward? In animal studies, selecting a reinforcer is not a standard difficulty, since food is used most frequently. By carefully reinforcing with food only desired responses, a hungry animal can be led to learn almost anything within its capabilities. This fact, however, is not as helpful as it might be when considering school learning. Unlike animal trainers, teachers are not in the position to make their students so hungry or thirsty that they will respond in order to receive a food pellet or a drink. Teachers instead have to look for some other kind of reinforcer, and thus the incessant search for ways to motivate students and control their learning.

In Skinner's view, the seriousness of this problem has been exaggerated. With proper arrangements, he maintains, the behavior of human beings can be shaped just as that of any other organism. In the article quoted above, he states that the three major shortcomings of current educational practice are:

1. The use of negative or aversive stimulation so that students engage in most of their activities in school in order to avoid criticism, punishment, low

* B. F. Skinner. The science of learning and the art of teaching. *Harv. educ. Rev.*, 1954, 24, pp. 86–87.
† W. C. H. Prentice. Some cognitive aspects of motivation. *Amer. Psychol.*, 1961, 16, 503–511.

marks, and the like. "In this welter of aversive consequences getting the right answer is in itself an insignificant event, any effect of which is lost amid the anxieties, the boredom, and the aggressions which are inevitable by-products of aversive control." *

2. Knowledge that a response is correct is adequate reinforcement, but in schools a pupil receives such reinforcement infrequently; and even when he does it is often delayed, thus reducing its value.

3. School instruction is not well programed. There is no carefully worked out sequence of steps such that each step makes the next one relatively simple, which would enable a pupil to receive reinforcement consistently as he progressively moves in the direction desired.

To meet these shortcomings of educational practice, Skinner proposed that schools make use of teaching machines or what have now come to be called programed materials. Figure 12 illustrates what Skinner had in mind, although without a machine. Materials of this sort are already in widespread use, and in general, results show that both children and adults can learn from such materials and that this learning appears to be at least as efficient as that from normal instructional procedures.

The role of reinforcement in these procedures is not without its ambiguities, however.† H. F. Silberman, with others, investigated three ways of presenting the materials in a logic lesson. The first was a fixed-sequence program using multiple-choice questions. The items were typed on cards and the subjects were told to think of the answer and then look at the correct answer on the back of the card. This covert responding contrasts with the constructed-response approach, used in Figure 12 but not in the Silberman study, in which the students write their answers. A branching group was permitted to back up one card at a time when they wanted to. A third group received the same material, except that the questions had been rewritten in paragraph form as statements with the answers filled in. Subjects in this textbook group were told to study the material in any way they wished. The subjects, paid high school students, were tested for both retention and for application or transfer of learning. The scores were highest in the textbook group, next for the branching group, and lowest in the fixed-sequence group.**

The authors conclude that the advantage of the textbook was the flexibility in sequence it permitted the student. If this is so, how does reinforcement enter in? What are the contingencies? They also concluded that it is better to give the student a "prompt" (that is, tell him the answer) before he makes his response than to confirm or reinforce a covert response after it has been made (it is assumed that students are prompted when reading a text). Most studies using constructed responses, however, have found confirmation better than prompting, but the results are not in perfect agreement. There are many other questions about programing not yet answered, partly because of the present imperfect understanding of reinforcement. Skinner maintains that

* B. F. Skinner. The science of learning, pp. 90–91.
† For a description of the various kinds of programs, see W. A. Deterline. An introduction to programed instruction. Englewood Cliffs, N. J.: Prentice-Hall, 1962.
** H. F. Silberman, R. E. Melaragno, J. E. Coulson, and D. Estavan. Fixed sequence versus branching autoinstructional methods. *J. educ. Psychol.,* 1961, 53, 165–172.

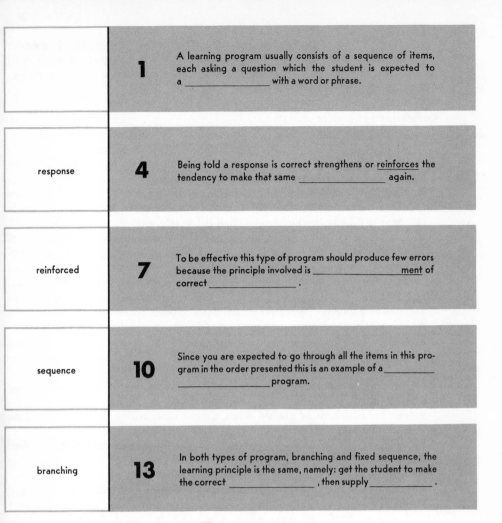

	1	A learning program usually consists of a sequence of items, each asking a question which the student is expected to a _____ with a word or phrase.
response	4	Being told a response is correct strengthens or <u>reinforces</u> the tendency to make that same _____ again.
reinforced	7	To be effective this type of program should produce few errors because the principle involved is _____ment of correct _____ .
sequence	10	Since you are expected to go through all the items in this program in the order presented this is an example of a _____ _____ program.
branching	13	In both types of program, branching and fixed sequence, the learning principle is the same, namely: get the student to make the correct _____ , then supply _____ .

Figure 12. An example of a brief learning program. Read item number 1 on this page and complete the statement with an appropriate word. Then turn to page 79 and check your answer. The second item is beside the answer to the first; after answering the second item go on to page 81 to check your answer— and for item 3. For checking item 3 and for the statement of item 4 return to this page. Proceed in this manner to the end of the program.

reinforcement must be almost immediate if it is to be effective. If that is the case, then how is the Bostrom study to be interpreted since the reinforcement was delayed for several weeks? In general, the functioning of reinforcement appears more clearly in animal than human learning. Many attempts to reproduce results of animal experiments with human beings, particularly in school learning, have not been fully successful.

These difficulties can be reduced by noting that reinforcement has two sorts of consequences. One may be described loosely as a motivating effect, the other as an increase in the information available to the student. Although both aspects of reinforcement are probably always present, the knowledge gained is probably the more important when a correct response is confirmed in a learning program, whereas the motivational influence is the more important when a lengthy sequence of behavior is reinforced.

Knowledge of Results

Knowledge of results enhances learning. On this point, research has been quite consistent. When a student obtains information about the adequacy of his responses, learning in almost all kinds of situations for all kinds of students is better than when it is lacking. Furthermore, the more immediate the knowledge of results the more reliable its effect on learning. Information concerning the adequacy of a single response is usually less ambiguous than being told, say, that a paper was good. What was good? All of it? The grammar? Every sentence, or just most of them? The ideas? All of them? An A on a paper is pleasant, but the information it gives is less directly useful than specific comments. Having a student chart his progress in arithmetic is helpful (especially when he is improving), but this outcome is more probably a result of increased motivation than of knowledge as such. The information given after a correct response not only strengthens that response but may provide direction for the next step. Since in school learning development of response sequences is usually more of a problem than strengthening a single response, this directive aspect of reinforcement is probably its most important function.

We have noted the value of immediate review and of active self-testing during learning. In each case, the individual is getting fairly immediate knowledge of where he stands, what he has done wrong, what he has done right, and where he needs to go next. One of the major differences between meaningful and meaningless materials is that with the former the student can tell if his response makes sense. If he understands, he can see that what he has been doing is sensible and consistent with prior learning, and further direction of his activity is fairly clear. In meaningless learning, right and wrong are arbitrary and unknown to the learner unless someone supplies that information. Thus, the more meaningful, well-structured, and organized the materials of learning can be made, the greater the degree to which learning can proceed under self-direction without the teacher's intervention.

In learning logical sequences, each step is dependent on the preceding one and thus is both the reinforcement for the preceding step and the stimulus for the next one. In doing a geometric proof the possibility of being able to take each step is reinforcing for the behavior involved in the preceding step, provided the process is understood. If the sequence of steps is mechanical, reinforcement must await some sort of check or teacher confirmation, which makes the possibility of error greater and hinders self-discovery of errors. This is one advantage of structural understanding over rote learning.

But not all materials are as well structured as geometry. The procedures for understanding a novel are not specified well enough for teachers to be able to count on appropriate self-reinforcement among students. Yet with this kind of material teachers usually can only reinforce specific responses occasionally. Does it follow that students acquire more correct responses in mathematics than in literature courses? Possibly. But it is also likely that

answer	**2**	As you can see, the correct response to the first item is the word "answer." A key feature of a program is the arrangement which tells a student immediately if the response he made was c_____ .
response	**5**	If, as Skinner claims, immediate reinforcement of correct responses is the key to learning, each item in an effective program should lead to the correct response so it can be immediately _____ed.
reinforcement responses	**8**	In the fixed sequence type of program used by Skinner, all students go through every item and in the same order. The program is arranged in small easy steps so that students will make very few _____ .
fixed sequence	**11**	In another type of program those who make errors either branch out to additional items or branch back to previous items to help them understand and correct their errors. Programs that have branches are called _____ing programs.
response reinforcement		

many students consider mathematics hard, not because they are expected to know more but because they are more aware of their shortcomings in the subject. Perhaps the challenge of hard work is an effective motivating device; certainly it is widely believed that a realistic assessment of one's knowledge and ability is a "good thing." Nevertheless, students who avoid courses and subjects they find hard have not as yet become an extinct species and there are even some who do not enjoy feeling inadequate.

MOTIVATION

Because of the motivational consequences cited above, a precise knowledge of results may be a mixed blessing. An individual may be disappointed or pleased, may be encouraged or discouraged. Worse yet, he may not care at all. For instance, in programed instruction the assumption is that the individual will read the items, will respond to the questions asked, and will be reinforced by being told whether he is right or wrong. However, neither the assumption that the individual will follow the directions and do what he is told, nor the assumption that obtaining knowledge of results will be satisfying is always true. What happens to learning when the individual just plain isn't interested? This is the motivational problem as teachers normally see it, with or without programed materials. How do you get students to want to do the things they are told to do and find pleasure in doing them? As everyone knows, the proper answer to this question is the unhelpful "It all depends." Most of the things on which "it" depends have already been discussed: drives, needs, and goals of students were considered in Chapter 2; teacher personality, environmental press, and learning materials were discussed in Chapter 3; and set, attitudes, and the law of effect in this chapter. However, these variables do not function independently of one another, and our discussion of the law of effect is still incomplete, since the motivating effects of reinforcement depend on the interactions between personality and situation.

Tasks and Motivation

Anxiety tests measure general drive level. If this level is very low, effort and awareness tend to be inadequate for efficient learning. Up to some point, increases in drive improve learning but thereafter they tend to interfere. Very strong anxiety may completely disrupt organized attempts to learn. The point of diminishing returns in anxiety level is a function of the complexity of the learning behavior required and of the amount of direction the situation provides the individual. The more difficult and complex the materials, the more likely it is that a high-anxious person will have trouble, because high anxiety tends to reduce flexibility and the ability to perceive alternatives. For example, anxiety is usually negatively related to test performance because most tests demand judgment and choice. Teachers can change the way anxiety affects learning by changing the task. They can make learning tasks more difficult and complex or simpler and less complex according to the amount of instruction and direction they give the student and according to the consistency and immediacy with which they supply knowledge of results. Anxiety tends to be a broad, general characteristic of an individual, but because it is learned, some situations are more anxiety-arousing than others for given individuals. Although anxiety level is an indication of the degree to which the individual is aroused or activiated, it is not an indication of the direction this activity will take. For this we need information concerning the individual's needs and goals.

These assertions may be illustrated by a study reported by J. Grimes and W. Allinsmith. In this study the interactions among a need, a drive, and two particular combinations of instructional procedure, environmental press, and materials are considered. One combination appeared in a "structured" school system, the other in the "unstructured" schools of another system. The structured schools began reading with the alphabet and used a systematic phonics program with drill separated from reading practice. Sounding out words was emphasized. In effect, in this school system the children were given a set of rules to follow in learning to read. In the structured schools, the classroom

correct	**3**	If the student responds to each item in order, he will immediately discover whether or not his r_____ is correct.
reinforced	**6**	By leading all students through the same fixed sequence of easy items a program should aid learning since each response made by the student will probably be correct and therefore can be _____ immediately.
errors or mistakes	**9**	A program may use multiple-choice recognition items or completion items like this one. In either case if every student must go through all the items in sequence, the program is called a fixed s_____ program.
branching	**12**	Typically, programs with multiple-choice items have a separate branch or set of items for each distractor (incorrect response) which explain the error before leading back to the main sequence of items. Thus multiple-choice items are most often used in the type called a _____ program.

atmosphere was found to be more authoritarian and cold and the curriculum more traditional. In the unstructured system reading instruction was based on the whole word, look-and-say approach, with incidental phonics starting at the end of the first grade. The teachers were more democratic and permissive; meaningful experience and "child expression" were emphasized. The adequacy of the procedure used to control other system differences is open to serious question, so a comparison of average achievement in the two systems is not justified.

Two personality measures were used. One was the Children's Anxiety Scale, an adaptation of the well-known Taylor Scale of Manifest Anxiety. This was given individually to each child by a trained examiner who helped the child in reading the items. The other measure was a rating scale of compulsivity. This scale gave high scores to children who were emotional or tense in disorganized situations and who worked very hard to achieve order and conformity with standards. These matters were not important to low scorers. The authors predicted that the compulsives with their low tolerance of ambiguity would perceive the unstructured whole-word reading program as disorganized and would have difficulty. They also predicted that the structured phonics approach should help the highly anxious child, although the measure of anxiety was unrelated to the measure of compulsivity. The criterion was over-all achievement on a standard test battery relative to predictions from IQ.

Figure 13 shows some of the results of this study. In the structured school

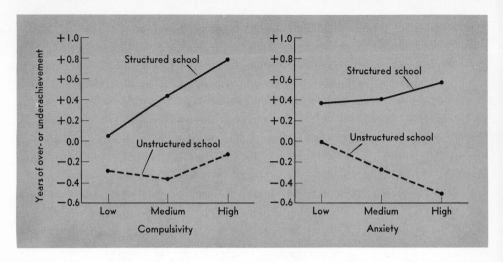

Figure 13. Mean school achievement relative to intelligence in two kinds of schools as a function of compulsivity and anxiety. (From J. Grimes and W. Allinsmith. Compulsivity, anxiety, and school achievement. Merrill-Palmer Quart., 1961, 7, 247–271.)

system compulsivity is positively related to achievement. The high compulsives achieve more than the low compulsives. In the other school system compulsivity and achievement are not related. The relationship of anxiety to achievement was low in the structured schools, but strongly negative in the unstructured schools. Considering the two motivational variables together, in the structured schools the high-compulsive, HA students did the best, with the high-compulsive, LA students standing second; it seems that need and the kind of materials available went hand in hand, and therefore high drive level was facilitating. High anxiety did not aid learning in the structured schools system compulsivity is positively related to achievement. The high compulsives LA students did the best, and the low-compulsive, HA students did the worst. Also, the high compulsives scored better on a phonics test than did the low compulsives. Compulsive students apparently tried to find a structure but the difficulty in doing so meant that high anxiety interfered with performance.

Naturally these results do not indicate how anxiety interacts with other needs and other kinds of learning situations. They merely illustrate the kind of relationships one may expect to find. They do, however, show that kind of motivation is a factor in a student's learning set. The high-compulsive children pay more attention to the structural aspects of the learning material, even when it is not particularly easy to do so, as evidenced by the greater knowledge of phonics among these children in the unstructured schools. This need to reduce ambiguity, to put things into an ordered and neat pattern, apparently produced a helpful set and facilitated transfer of the phonics materials to reading achievement; it does not of course follow that it facilitates all kinds of transfer since its effectiveness appears limited to material susceptible to neat packaging. Thus needs influence learning by influencing set, that is, needs tend to direct a person's attention toward certain aspects of learning materials and predispose him to put them together in certain ways.

The Grimes and Allinsmith study also illustrates that an important factor in teaching methods is the matter of selecting, organizing, and arranging the materials. The structure of the content chosen limits the kinds of contingencies for reinforcement that it is possible to arrange. A particular arrangement is more likely to be effective with some students than with others because differences in needs create differences in the motivating effects of the reinforcement that can be given.

Reward and Punishment

It has been known for some time that the motivating effects of rewards and punishments vary from one individual to the next, particularly when, as is so often the case, the amount of information provided by the reward or punishment is low. After all, the clarity of the information given to a student by a single course grade, a test score, or a mark on a paper is limited. The student may infer many things from a mark ("What a stupid and unreasonable teacher!") that may or may not be what the teacher meant to communicate. In some cases marks elicit more activity from students, but by themselves they offer few suggestions as to what this activity should be. Although an A+ is probably gratifying to any student and an F is not, the motivational consequences of most grades are difficult to predict. A grade of C will be rewarding or punishing to a student depending on his level of aspiration—that is, on his expectations, his needs, the pressures on him, the grades others receive, and the like. A student with a strong achievement need or any other strong need relevant to grades (such as recognition) who is told in detail about his errors may find this information unpleasant, no matter how helpful.

Here is one of the basic difficulties of reward and punishment systems for the motivation of learning. For the truly successful students who are continuously rewarded there is no problem. They are doing well, they know it, they know that others know it, and all they have to do is to keep on doing the same thing. For others, matters are not so simple. Objective and complete information concerning progress helps a student learn. Yet when given this information the student knows just where he stands, and under these circumstances a student can only be rewarded realistically for doing well compared to his past performance. To the poor student such a "reward" may merely mean that if this level is considered good for him he can never really do very well. Furthermore, good students can reasonably expect greater praise than poor students, even when their performance is not an improvement. Thus, a precise and objective system of marking, in which attempts are made to reward achievement, will be punishing to many students, to some almost continuously. A less objective system may reward effort more often, but if the student really knows where he stands the rewarding effects may be small. In short, a reward system tends to run afoul of the requirement that the student receive knowledge of results.

Implicit in the preceding discussion is the notion that punishment is not an effective motivating device. Actually, little is known about the role of punishment in human learning. It is generally agreed that punishment arouses anxiety, creates tension, and leads to efforts to escape. But what an individual learns from the punishment is hard to predict. There are two reasons for this difficulty. First, punishment is not an efficient means of transmitting information. When given after a long sequence of responses, it only informs the individual that something was wrong; under similar circumstances, reward is not very efficient, either. However, reward of a single response does tell him that that response was correct; but punishment of that response, while saying that it was wrong, may not tell the individual what to do. The second general difficulty in predicting the effects of punishment stems from the anxiety and emotion created. The anxiety aroused is easily attached to the entire situation. When the punishment administered is severe, or when it is administered frequently even though mildly, the whole learning situation may become something to avoid.

Repeated punishment or threat of punishment will suppress a response, but unless some other satisfactory response is learned in its place this suppression may not be permanent, especially if the response was reinforced sometime prior to its punishment. When whole behavior sequences are punished, because of the tendency for punishment effects to generalize, the effect, even if the individual knows what was wrong, may be to suppress many responses, not just those for which the punishment was administered. Reaction to punishment is usually an attempt to escape. Any substitute response made and not punished is, in effect, reinforced since it constitutes escape. If each wrong attempt is punished and the correct response is not made, tension and anxiety will continue to mount and the net result may be complete disorganization of behavior.

Therefore, if punishment is going to be useful three conditions must be met. First, escape or avoidance behavior must be prevented unless that is the learning desired. Avoidance behavior is anxiety-reducing and therefore automatically self-reinforcing. Secondly, punishment should be followed immediately by information on how to proceed so that a correct response may be promptly reinforced. Otherwise, tension will continue to increase and efforts to escape will be even stronger. Thirdly, the punishment should be mild so that the degree of anxiety aroused is not too great. In school situations escape behavior is usually punished and students can avoid this punishment by not trying to escape from school. By and large, this is an effective device. But if learning situations in school are also punishing, then all of school becomes highly anxiety-arousing, and even temporary escapes may be strongly reinforcing. It is certainly not surprising that the academic records of school dropouts (the more than 1,000,000 children who quit school each year) tend to be quite poor.

In our schools good academic grades tend to be considered rewards and poor academic grades tend to be considered punishment. Of course, not all children by any means find a mark of C or D particularly distressing. And not all students find A's particularly rewarding. But since grades are administered according to achievement rather than need for achievement, it can be seen why educators sometimes urge that grades be de-emphasized or eliminated. Most teachers at all levels deplore the fact that many students work for grades rather than in order to learn, and they frequently suggest substituting another system. Some school systems have changed their marking system a dozen times in almost as many years in an attempt to escape the dilemma. Apparently those who recommend these changes, while sensitive to the problems created by marks, do not understand the nature of the difficulty. If only because of the value system of our society, some sort of motivational consequence is an inevitable result of the necessary steps in supplying knowledge of results in school learning. It may be noted in passing that the values referred to are particularly those of the middle class, but since middle-class values are dominant in our society and very particularly dominant in our schools, even lower-class children who come from a background where academic achievement is not highly valued find low grades punishing.

If we accept as inevitable that assessment of achievement has motivating consequences, there is no reason why a standard grading system can't serve as well as any other. In general, the amount of specific information given should be as great as possible, since this will provide direction for further learning. But any device that leads to further efforts, rather than to attempts to avoid or escape learning, may prove helpful. To accomplish this is not always difficult, as a study by E. B. Page demonstrates.

The students of 74 randomly selected secondary school teachers were divided into three groups, also in a random fashion. Each teacher gave his class an objective test of his own choosing which fit into the usual course of instruction and graded the test in his usual manner. The teachers made no comments on the papers of one group; to a second group they made any comments they considered appropriate for that student on that test; for the third group, the experimenter specified that the teacher make the following comments:

A — "Excellent, keep it up"
B — "Good work, keep at it"
C — "Perhaps try to do still better?"
D — "Let's bring this up"
F — "Let's raise this grade"

The papers were then returned to the students. The three groups were compared on their performance on the next objective test each teacher chose to give. The results of this study are shown in Table 12. The free-comment group did the best and the no-comment group the worst. The effects on the F students were significantly stronger than among the other students.

Page concluded, "When the average secondary teacher takes the time and trouble to write comments (believed to be 'encouraging') on student papers, these apparently have a measurable and potent effect upon student effort, or attention, or attitude, or whatever it is which causes learning to improve, and this effort does not appear dependent on school building, school year, or student ability." It seems reasonable to believe that this "whatever it is that causes learning to improve" is arousal of a motive. Any of several motives seem likely candidates: (a) need for achievement, (b) need for recognition, in this case the hope to elicit further attention and comment from the teacher, and (c) need for affiliation, such as desire to please the teacher.

TABLE 12

Effect of Comments on Performance as Indicated by Letter Grades [a]

	Comment Groups		
Letter Grade	No Comment	Free Comment	Specified Comment
A	1.93	2.04	2.03
B	1.91	2.11	1.98
C	1.90	2.06	2.04
D	2.05	1.99	1.96
F	1.57	2.55	1.88
All grades	1.91	2.09	2.01

Adapted from E. B. Page. Teacher comments and student performance: a seventy-four classroom experiment in school motivation. *J. educ. Psychol.*, 1958, 49, 173–181.

[a] Sets of three students in a given class, one in each comment group, receiving the same initial grade were ranked on final test (1 = lowest, 3 = highest). The mean rank of each group was found for each class. The means above are means of these means.

In any case, it seems apparent that appropriate comments can improve the motivating effect of grades and in particular can mitigate undesirable effects of failure grades.

Although grades are one of the most prominent consequences of student performance, they are far from the only devices teachers use. Especially for long behavior sequences, the choice of a consequence may be quite arbitrary and can be switched from one thing to another by the teacher, who may say to the students, "If you finish this set of arithmetic problems you may then read a book," thereby making reading the reinforcement for finishing the arithmetic. Under such circumstances reading a book is usually considered a privilege by the students. There is no logical reason why the situation cannot be reversed. A teacher may say, "If you finish reading that book, then you can work on your arithmetic." Although tradition has it that free reading is more satisfying than doing arithmetic, if the teacher regularly made doing arithmetic the privilege and reading a book the work, it is quite possible that many students would learn to consider arithmetic a very satisfying activity, and it could serve as reinforcement for the reading behavior.

But even if the students did not develop attraction towards arithmetic, receiving this "reinforcement" could serve several kinds of needs because working on arithmetic would become a signal to all concerned that success had been achieved in reading. We need not argue whether needs are learned or innate in order to agree that ways of satisfying needs are learned and that a given consequence of behavior may serve different needs for different individuals.

In short, it is by arranging and controlling the consequences of behavior that teachers make use of pupil motivation to direct learning. The more certain and direct their control of these consequences, the more certain and direct will be their control of learning. Direct arousal of a particular need permits the greatest control, but use of consequences that may serve any one of several possibly aroused needs is often a satisfactory substitute. But unfortunately, or perhaps fortunately, teachers do not have full control of the consequences of student behavior even in their own classrooms. Many of these consequences occur outside the classroom, particularly in the home from parents. As a student grows older reinforcement from other students becomes an increasingly major force.

Motivation in Classroom Groups

A classrooom is an organized social group with many lines of social action between individuals. Students reinforce and motivate each other; also, they instruct each other both directly and by providing models for imitation. It is not unusual in some classrooms for the positive reinforcement offered a student by his classmates when he talks out of turn to be so strong that teacher disapproval merely adds zest to the game. In other classes the students not only surround disruptive behavior with disapproval but actively reinforce one another's learning. Even ignoring all the consequences a student's behavior may bring outside the immediate classroom situation, the number of possible reinforcement patterns is very large. Essentially the variables affecting these patterns are those that produce the environmental press characteristic of the school generally and the class in particular. The individual student's personality will of course create variations within the general pattern.

It follows from this last fact that the kinds of similarities and diversities created by homogeneous or heterogeneous groupings will affect the way in which a class or a group functions. E. P. Torrance studied groups of five students working together on a task. In two schools homogeneous groups were formed by putting together the five pupils in the class ranking highest on a measure of creativity, the next five in a second group, and so on. In another school the same procedure was followed using intelligence test scores to sort out the groups. Heterogeneous groups were made in other classes by ranking the students and then taking every fifth student for group I and so forth. The groups' task was to think of as many uses as they could for each of a collection of science toys (nutty putty, a magnet, and so on) and to explain the principle behind these uses. Each group worked for 25 minutes in a separate room closely watched by a trained observer who recorded the instances of positive and negative interactions. The kinds of behavior considered positive were: cooperating, organizing, absorption in task, praising one another, and so on. Negative instances included bickering, dominating, squelching, reprimanding, refusal to cooperate, and loss of interest.

In each school the number of positive interactions was significantly greater in the homogeneous groups than in the heterogeneous groups (see Figure 14). Nevertheless, the homogeneous groups were not more effective than the heterogeneous groups. In one of the schools divided according to creativity the homogeneous groups were a bit more productive of ideas than the heterogeneous groups, but in the other school so divided there was no such tendency. In the school divided by intelligence contradictory trends at different levels of in-

School
Learning

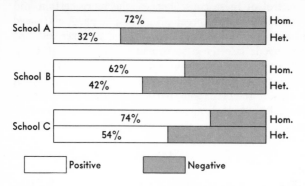

Figure 14. Interactions during science-toy task. In schools A and B grouping was based on a test of imagination; in school C on an intelligence test. (Adapted from E. P. Torrance. Can grouping control social stress in creative activities? El. Sch. J., 1961, 62, 139–149.)

telligence were found. This result seems perfectly reasonable. Although the students in the homogeneous groups received more positive reinforcement from one another, not all the ideas or responses being reinforced were necessarily useful ones. Furthermore, the greater amount of tension in the heterogeneous groups may have raised the general drive level of some subjects. Any of the heterogeneous groups containing individuals with the appropriate abilities and motivational set could have profited from this increased drive in spite of the interference created for other individuals in the group, since in this task one individual may be able to produce for the benefit of all.

Given either a different kind of task or some other basis for grouping, the results would probably have been altered. Group size is another relevant variable. When groups get quite large a majority of the group may become more or less inactive, and it becomes necessary for one or more individuals to assume leadership roles. These people then become major sources of reinforcement.

In the typical classroom, of course, the teacher usually assumes this leadership role. But even in the most rigidly run classrooms of the raise-your-hand-before-you-can-speak type, reinforcement of student by student is frequent albeit not always helpful. Probably any teacher who insists students talk only to him must exercise great vigilance and skill to maintain these rules. Some teachers who attempt to function this way find themselves spending all their time in this activity, some simply fail. Probably these teachers do not last very long, the former because they find the strain too great and the latter because nobody appreciates teachers who cannot manage their classrooms. Still other teachers run tightly controlled classrooms but without the use of aversive techniques. These teachers apparently use techniques of positive reinforcement but not just of the type discussed so far. These are the teachers who make the work exciting and interesting and who arouse the curiosity of the students about the task at hand. W. C. H. Prentice, in the article quoted earlier in this chapter (see p. 75), suggested that the cognitive experiences associated with novelty, surprise, change, difficulty, unpredictability, and clarity can have reinforcing properties. Nevertheless, no matter how skillful a teacher may be, at times the forces of social approval or disapproval may require that students reject reinforcement of this sort.

In many schools in this country, the student who permits himself to become too deeply involved in academic achievement gets few immediate external rewards for his behavior. It should be added that academic failure and total ignorance frequently bring disapproval from other students, as well as from teachers and parents. Nevertheless, the most effective routes to social approval are typically athletic prowess and participation in school activities. Furthermore, teachers and the general community tend to perpetuate these patterns. In many cases teachers respond most positively to the socially powerful students in their classes while shaking their heads over the maladjustment of students who are not well-accepted. Sometimes schools or individual teachers use or try to use these group pressures to achieve their ends. Making eligibility for athletic and other nonacademic activities dependent upon grades is one simple example. Setting up group competitions is a standard technique of getting students not only to reward and punish each other but also to teach each other.*

The motivational currents of the sort just discussed and the patterns of reinforcement that accompany them are only part of the story, and the strength of these variables can be overestimated. Important but not considered here are the effects on other students of a teacher's interaction with one student, and the effects on teacher behavior of student actions. Students reward and punish teacher behavior both deliberately and incidentally. Still, teachers are in a position of authority in schools, and this authority is for the most part respected. It is in some ways rather surprising but nonetheless true that by and large students in the overwhelming majority of instances do pretty much what teachers tell them to.

The motivational patterns stemming from the students' group membership is only another one of the factors we have discussed in this chapter that determine the direction and amount of learning activity. A student's expectations of the rewards and punishments that a given sort of school performance entails is a kind of knowledge that tends to generate and direct activity. Learning materials have the same sort of effect, so do teachers' instructions and directions, so do the students' developed abilities and prior knowledge of the material. All this does not mean that ability, knowledge, attitude, and need are the same thing, only that their influence on set is similar. In many cases these internal variables will conflict with one another just as they may conflict with external influences on set. However, it is in these similarities in effect on learning set that teachers' opportunities to influence learning largely occur. To increase the range, level, and scope of students' abilities is usually the ultimate goal. To accomplish this end teachers provide students with information in various guises. They present learning materials, they tell and show students what to do and how to do it, they point to goals and provide incentives, and they supply knowledge of results and other sorts of reinforcement. These teacher actions influence the course of learning largely through their influence on students' learning sets.

* Bronfenbrenner has described the elaborate use of this technique in Russian schools. U. Bronfenbrenner. Soviet methods of character education: some implications for research. *Amer. Psychol.*, 1962, 17, 550–564.

Instructional Procedures

The materials presented in the preceding chapters carry with them many rather obvious corollaries concerning the procedures a teacher should use in instruction, and it is difficult to resist the temptation to make a long list of these truisms and generalizations—some of which have already been offered. But before we further succumb to this temptation, we should look at the research on teaching methods, because no matter how obvious the conclusions to be drawn about teaching from the ideas already discussed may seem, the following statements, offered by R. M. W. Travers, are equally well supported.

90

5

1. Differences in achievement of pupils exposed to different teaching methods are small and not generally consistent from study to study.

2. The method considered to be the experimental method in particular studies tends to show some slight superiority to the method described as the control method.

3. When teachers are asked to teach two classes by different methods, the teachers show only limited capacity for changing their pattern of behavior as they switch from method to method. This fact may account for the small differences between methods found in some of the studies.

4. Very few studies provide data indicating the way in which one method of teaching differs from another. Research workers usually report how the methods are *alleged* to differ, but few studies provide data indicating how the methods *actually* differ in terms of the recorded behavior of the teachers in the classroom.*

Travers concludes that therefore the reasons for the few differences that are found cannot be determined. He adds that in most studies the common textbooks, practice exercises, and the like used by all groups may mask differences resulting from methods.

Since many of the studies cited in the preceding chapters demonstrate that the actions of the teacher (or experimenter) do matter, there seems to be a paradox: Many variables under teacher control influence student learning, yet studies of teaching methods have had the results just described. Three considerations explain the discrepancy. First, with a few exceptions, the studies of learning have measured specific and immediate outcomes, whereas the methods studies tend to measure general growth in a subject area. Second, studies of learning usually examine student practice activity while, except for some of the recent work with programing, the methods studies have rarely described student activity, much less tried to control it. Instead, the effects of teacher action on student activity have usually been assumed or ignored.

Third, the word "method" is vague. It may be helpful here to distinguish between what may be called "teaching techniques" and "educational methods." Investigations of educational methods compare approaches that differ in the immediate goals of instruction and in the content presented as well as, or instead of, the teacher's technique. Many of the people who engage in arguments about methods in education try to "prove" their choice is "best" on the basis of research and psychological argument, overlooking the fact that choices of content and goals must ultimately be decided on philosophical grounds. Not so with teaching techniques. In a study of teaching technique the ways in which teachers attempt to influence student activity would be examined, using the same content for the same purposes and with the intention of getting students to engage in the same practice. The success of a technique would be measured directly by the degree to which desired practice was produced, or indirectly by a learning measure.

* R. M. W. Travers. *Essentials of learning.* New York: Macmillan, 1963, p. 4.

Method and Achievement

When well done, studies of educational method can nevertheless provide valuable information about what to teach if not about how to teach. A study of teaching subtraction in grade three reported by W. A. Brownell and H. E. Moser is an example.* They compared achievement among students taught to subtract by means of decomposition (D) or by means of equal additions (EA). To subtract 35 from 73 by decomposition the student thinks $13 - 5 = 8$, $6 - 3 = 3$, result is 38; he has "borrowed" 10 from the seven tens. To subtract by equal additions he thinks $13 - 5 = 8$, $7 - 4 = 3$, result is 38; he has added 10 to both numbers. Both are standard methods in widespread use.

Half of the students learning D and half of those learning EA had instruction characterized as rational or meaningful; for the remainder the instruction was described as mechanical. The meaningful instruction attempted to get students to understand the reasons for the subtraction method they were learning to use. In the mechanical approaches, pat verbal formulas were given in answer to questions about why the method worked, and the emphasis was on repetitive drill. Hence, two kinds of content and two kinds of practice were used, so that four different methods result: decomposition taught rationally (DR), decomposition taught mechanically (DM), equal additions taught rationally (EAR), and equal additions taught mechanically (EAM).

Three weeks of training using these methods were given to approximately 1300 third grade pupils in four different school systems. In the 12 classes in the first system, called Center A, the pupils had had during grades one and two considerable systematic work in arithmetic emphasizing meaningful experiences. Center B consisted of 12 classes from a school system in which there was much talk about meaningful arithmetic in the first two grades but little practice of it. There was, however, much computational training during this period in Center B. The two other school systems made up Center C and contained 17 classes. The pupils in these schools had had little arithmetic instruction before the third grade and most of that was of an abstract, mechanical nature. Each center was treated separately, and the four groups in each center were roughly matched in ability and initial achievement. The different teaching procedures were outlined to volunteer teachers who chose the method they wished to employ in their classes.

The same number of practice exercises and the same materials were used by all groups, but the work for one of the 15 days was not specified on the assumption that the M sections would use it for drill and the R sections to make up for the longer explanations required for their procedures. End tests and six-week retention tests measuring speed, accuracy, and transfer

*W. A. Brownell and H. E. Moser. *Meaningful vs. mechanical learning: a study in grade III subtraction*. Duke University Research Studies in Education, No. 8. Durham, N. C.: Duke University Press, 1949.

were given. From interviews it was determined that the children understood decomposition more readily than equal additions, but that in both cases the rational approach led to more understanding than the mechanical method, as of course it should.

With respect to accuracy, the DR method appeared uniformly superior on the end test, and also on the retention and transfer tests except at Center A. With respect to speed, however, the equal additions technique appears to be about as good as the decomposition procedure and it was best at Center A. The center differences are probably the effects of prior training, but it is difficult to specify just what aspect of the variations in previous training are the important ones. Some help comes from comments, in the teachers' diaries from Center A, which indicated that the M groups were dissatisfied at first with the teachers' "explanations" but after two or three days accepted the verbal formulas used with no further comments. The records from Center C, where the children had no background of meaningful arithmetic, showed no signs of the initial resistance evident in Center A. Perhaps for the same reasons, the children in Center A showed a greater tendency to attempt rationalization of the rules they were taught in the M sections than did those from Center C. Thus, a difference in set created by type of prior training seems to be involved.

The different procedures also show to different advantage according to criterion (accuracy or speed, direct learning or transfer) and by timing of the test (immediate post-test or six-week retention test). This lack of uniformity in results creates a sticky problem that is unfortunately common. The problem is that few methods are uniformly best or worst. The determination of "best" depends on value choices which usually require compromise. It is common for schoolmen to argue that transfer criteria are most useful. Although this is a reasonable view it raises still further problems. One in particular is quite thorny and stems from the role of intelligence in transfer.

Method and Intelligence

Bright pupils use prior learning more readily than dull pupils, and therefore in complex sequential learning, differences in performance according to intelligence are usually obvious and large. However, when learning tasks do not require much transfer of prior learning or transfer within the sequence currently being learned, the differences in performance between bright and dull are reduced or disappear. Anything that will help produce the desired set in a student should also reduce his need for ability. One example is the organizer used by Ausubel and Fitzgerald; the learning of a group given an organizer showed a lower relationship to ability than did the learning of a group not given the organizer passage (see p. 71).

In many respects a similar idea underlies the procedures in the construction of a program. Careful sequential arrangements make transfer of prior steps in the sequence easier. Immediate reinforcement of responses adds further clarity. Therefore, careful programing of materials reduces the role that intelligence plays in learning. Or to put it the other way around, when a careful sequence is not set up, a learning task becomes a puzzle and it takes more intelligence to solve that puzzle. For this reason, the learning of well-programed materials should show a lower relationship to intelligence than do poorly programed materials.

Now just this relationship has been found in several studies of programed versus nonprogramed instruction. In the study by Silberman and others which was cited earlier (see p. 76) the correlations between post-test score, aptitude, and time differed among the groups as shown in Table 13. Ability was most closely related to test performance in the textbook group, which also had the highest test scores, but speed was most closely related to aptitude in the fixed-sequence group. Speed and score were not related. There are other studies in which similar relationships between intelligence and achievement have appeared, which at the same time have found higher average scores for the group using the programed materials.

TABLE 13

Correlations of Aptitude,
Training Time, and Post-test Scores

Variables Correlated	Group		
	Fixed-Sequence	Back-Branching	Text-book
Aptitude versus score	.45	.39	.67 [b]
Aptitude versus time	—.52 [a]	—.45	—.31
Time versus score	—.14	.03	—.04

From H. F. Silberman, R. E. Melaragno, J. E. Coulson, and D. Estavan. Fixed sequence versus branching autoinstructional methods. *J. educ. Psychol.*, 1961, 53, 165–172. Research sponsored by System Development Corporation.

[a] $P < .05$.
[b] $P < .01$.

Figure 15 illustrates one way in which these results may have come about. These data can be interpreted in two ways. One can say that it is possible to so organize and structure learning materials, and arrange reinforcements by putting the materials in the proper sequence that learning becomes easy. So hooray for programed instruction! On the other hand one may describe these procedures as arranging matters so that the learners do not have to use and practice their learning abilities. Looked at in this way the advantages of programing seem less obvious; to program the materials may reduce practice of the kind that one really wanted the students to have. Thus, an approach that requires an individual to develop new abilities may be less efficient for the acquisition of the knowledge than one that requires the use of already stabilized abilities such as reading and filling in blanks, yet it may be more efficient for other ends. Example: A course in psychology may help teachers directly by enabling them to talk intelligently (or impressively) to parents about learning but help much less with their instruction. Conversely, direct instruction and practice in teaching may be an inefficient way of acquiring knowledge about learning but quite effective in improving teaching skill. Thus, the objective of developing certain abilities may conflict with the objective of acquiring knowledge. Of course by taking more time both may be accomplished, but longer periods of training will not solve all problems, because as learning proceeds in a given area the abilities involved may change.

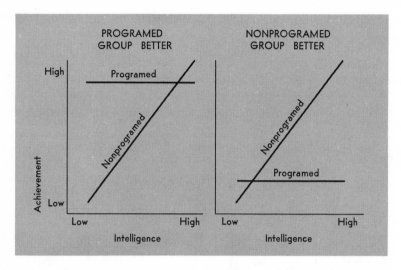

Figure 15. Possible relationships between intelligence and achievement for groups using programed and nonprogramed material. The exaggerated schematic relationships shown above indicate that programing could reduce or eliminate intelligence as a factor in learning by helping slow students as on the left, hindering bright students as on the right, or both.

For example, L. W. Towner analyzed the performance of medical students on a test of knowledge about cancer. He found that from the freshman to senior year the factors measured by the test changed gradually from specific, academic, factual knowledge to organized, clinical knowledge. Differences in test scores among freshmen and sophomores were largely in quantity of facts known. Differences among seniors were more typically in the degree of generality and organization of this knowledge.* In an extension of this study, the differences in performance on the same test among students taking various kinds of special courses in cancer were examined. Group discussions, opportunities to observe doctors working with patients, and a chance to work with patients themselves were among the kinds of special courses offered. Sophomores apparently profited from the observations, but this was not true for juniors and seniors. In fact, the juniors who worked with patients and also took the observation courses did less well on the examination than those doing only the clinical work. Group discussions were associated with the

* L. W. Towner. A factorial investigation of medical students' knowledge of cancer at different levels of training. *Educ. psychol. Measmt.*, 1957, 17, 115–130.

highest-scoring groups among the seniors but not among those in the lower classes. The authors concluded that among the seniors the effective courses ". . . helped students organize and integrate their knowledge about cancer. The approaches not well adapted to this purpose appeared inefficient." Table 14 indicates the shifts in effect of the courses on achievement over the last three years of medical school.

TABLE 14

Effect of Various Types of Course Work on Knowledge of Cancer among Medical Students

Type of Course	Effect among		
	Sophomores	Juniors	Seniors
Discussions	None	None	Strongly positive, especially in conjunction with working with patients
Observing work with patients	Positive	Negative when working with patients also, otherwise none	None
Working with patients	Not used	Positive except when combined with observation	Positive

Adapted from D. R. Green and L. W. Towner. The relation of medical school teaching methods to student performance on a test of cancer knowledge. *J. nat. cancer Inst.,* 1959, 23, 605–616.

It will suprise no one that as students get fairly advanced in an area, approaches that permit them greater freedom and self-direction in their learning become increasingly helpful. Nor should it be suprising that exchanging information with one's peers, once a substantial amount of knowledge is acquired, is also effective. Both of these conclusions have been widely recognized for a long time. The seminar and the independent investigation have been the central part of graduate education for many years. However, the freer a student becomes to pursue learning in his own way, the greater difficulty the psychologist has in determining how learning is proceeding. And there is every reason to believe it proceeds in different ways among different individuals. This inference follows from the fact noted several times previously, that whenever external direction in a situation is low, personality factors become stronger influences on activity.

An example of the com-
plexities this creates can be seen in a study in which all students in an
elementary psychology course attended two lectures a week and two section
meetings a week. For two weeks of the semester the regular lecture-discussion
sections were discontinued, and half the class met in small groups while the
other half wrote papers. Later in the semester the procedure was repeated,
reversing the groups. A variety of personality measures, ratings, grades, and
observation records were used. Measures of n Affiliation and self-reliance were
found to be unrelated to student satisfaction or performance, involvement in
the small groups, or independent study. The n Achievement measure gave the
results shown in Table 15 for women. Those at the high end of the scale
preferred the two variations in procedures while those in the middle preferred
the lectures. Among the men no significant differences according to n Achievement scores were found. On a measure of need for power (obtained in a
fashion similar to n Achievement), high-scoring women participated in the
small group discussions to a lesser degree than women with low n Power
scores. This time just the reverse was found for men.

TABLE 15

Relationship between Women's Need for Achievement and Teaching Method Preferences

	Preference for Method		
Need for Achievement	Lecture	Small Group	Inde-pendent
High	2	8	5
Mid	16	4	3
Low	7	7	6

From K. Koenig and W. J. McKeachie. Personality and independent study. *J. educ.
Psychol.*, 1959, 50, 132–134.

Although the authors report that a second study indicated students who
think the instructor should be authoritarian tend to do poorly in independent
study, a number of other investigations have failed to find any differences
among groups who have and have not been allowed to follow the procedure
they preferred. Thus, personality influences both preferences for methods
and the activities a method elicits, but preferences are related to achievement only some of the time.

The numerous studies of lecture versus discussion versus independent
study for college students have failed more often than not to produce important differences in achievement. In the face of the sort of conflicting needs
among students just illustrated, it is difficult to see how a teacher, even one
who knew his students well, could make intelligent choices of instructional
procedures according to student personality; it is easy to see, however, why

the effects of the teacher's choice of method so often balance out, so that the net result is no difference between groups taught by different procedures.

In almost all the studies of educational method, the different groups studied different materials or topics and engaged in different kinds of practice activities. It is highly probable that some of these variations in method forced the teachers to use different techniques in getting the students to practice as planned, because questions about teaching technique are not entirely independent of those about educational method. Nevertheless, once a decision about method (objectives, content, materials, and kind of student practice wanted) has been made, questions about technique remain. For instance, a standard aspect of a teacher's task is to judge the degree to which adequate learning has occurred at a given point and to decide how much more practice in what context is needed for retention and understanding by students. Repetition in varied settings enhances both retention and understanding, but these decisions are part of educational method rather than technique. Suppose that a history teacher, having read student papers on the political antecedents of World War I, judges it advisable to ask for another set of papers on the economic antecedents of the same war from some of his students and for a paper parallel to the first one about World War II from other students. The teacher's decisions would be based on his opinion of the knowledge and abilities his students needed to develop, but the amount and kind of guidance he gives each student (that is, his technique) could vary quite substantially over and above this choice. Thus, regardless of topic, some students could be turned loose with only the direction to go write a paper, while others could be given very specific instructions about how to proceed. They could be told how to search for material, each item in their outline could be checked, and so on. This independence of method and technique is not complete since the decision to have papers written precludes certain kinds of teacher control, unless one were willing to consider having a teacher direct and approve the writing of each word, a technique that might prove fatal to the sanity of teacher and student alike.

The basic principle involved in teaching techniques is that regardless of what a teacher does it is the student's activities that determine the course of learning. Having determined what he wants his students to do, half the teacher's task is done. This half calls for choices among methods. The remaining half is to get the students to do it. As a rule, this can be accomplished in a wide variety of ways, and there is no reason to assert that one teaching technique is better than another, provided students in fact carry on the desired activity.

Instruction can be described as the direction of learning by changing set. A teaching technique is a particular way of manipulating the factors under teacher control that influence set. Teaching techniques may vary in the ways they (1) arouse motives, (2) direct student attention to the elements of the materials and content and to the objectives of the instruction, (3) guide students' practice procedures, and (4) provide reinforcement and knowledge of results. In some cases teachers may go through each of these steps for nearly every step a student takes. Thus, a teacher might say, "To get a good grade you should learn how to take these raw scores and convert them to grade equivalent scores so you can see that the shape of the distribution is altered by this change in scale. Look at the first score. Now see that number in Column I of the table and note the corresponding number in Column II. That's right. Now . . ." With less structured and organized techniques, various portions of these steps may be omitted or left implicit. Teachers may rely on other cues in a situation to arouse motives, they may let students discover for themselves the nature of the materials and they may leave the objectives vague or entirely up to the student to determine—although at least this latter is probably rare. They may guide student practice by telling them what to do, by showing them how to do it, by pointing to a model or by relying on the already developed abilities of the student. They may provide reinforcement or let students find their own sources for reinforcement.

For the investigation of techniques, information about the cues, directions, and reinforcements occurring in relationship to student activity must be obtained. Since it is evidently desirable that students have considerable freedom to control their own learning in the later stages of progress in any given area, the investigation of teaching techniques at this level is hampered. However, some crude but potentially effective devices have been known for a long time. For example, students can be asked to describe or keep notes about their activities as they proceed with their learning. Classes can be filmed and taped. Students can be shown these films or hear these tapes and can be asked what they were thinking about or doing at a given moment. It should be possible to analyze the notes and drafts as well as the final versions of papers that students write. The small handful of studies of this sort that have been done indicate that some valuable information could be acquired using such techniques, but they are too few in number for any generalizations to be made at the moment.

For the most part, what is known about techniques is so painfully obvious that it is rarely discussed. You want a student to learn about the federal government? Tell him about it, or give him a book about it and tell him to read it. Although this sort of procedure is hardly all one can do in teaching, sometimes it is quite enough. Most of the research on effective teaching techniques has taken place under circumstances of substantial external control and direction of student activity. There are on the one hand the studies of learning of the sort reported in Chapter 4, which are difficult to generalize to the classroom since many of them involve special situations and very short periods of time. Beyond this there are the many recent studies of programed instruction. While there are few inherent limitations to the programing procedure as a device for studying instructional techniques, the work that has been done to date is relatively limited. Not only have the kinds of programs in use been of the sort that control every step of the way for students—leaving them little of the flexibility that the Silberman study suggests may sometimes be desirable—but also for the most part the objectives of the programs have been the acquisition of knowledge. The abilities developed have been limited primarily to increased skill in following standard programs. Still, these devices, especially when used with some of the more elaborate hardware—computer systems and the like—offer the possibility of reasonably controlled studies of how the external forces influencing set may be manipulated during the protracted learning sequences characteristic of school learning.* Thus, while traditional procedures, regular books, and the like may continue to dominate the educational scene because they are as yet unexcelled for many purposes, the use of explicitly programed materials permits the study of school instruction in a fashion heretofore almost impossible.

Someday it may be even possible to teach teachers how to teach as well as what to teach. Current instruction in teaching methods is done mostly by example and apprenticeship and therefore depends on the competence of the models provided and the ease of imitation of these models. This may be one reason methods courses in education departments are apparently so ineffective. The information about teaching techniques in these courses is usually based on lore, gimmicks, and theories whose relation to fact is unknown. This lack of knowledge may also explain why in many of these courses more attention is given to the objectives, materials, and nature of the subject matter the student will teach than to techniques.

In general, most arguments about teaching are not about techniques of instruction but about what students should learn. That these arguments have often been labeled arguments about how-to-do-it has merely served to confuse matters. For example, the arguments about teaching reading that have raged for so long have focused on the question of where phonics fits appropriately into such instruction. A method of teaching reading that includes phonics differs from a method that does not. Unquestionably, this difference in content produces different learning. But until agreement can be reached about the degree to which the knowledge and skills involved in learning phonics enter into learning to read at various stages of that learning, such arguments will continue. Thus, it is to be expected that these heated arguments concerning educational method will continue for some time. In the meantime, most teachers will continue to get students to learn to read by hook or by crook. Their methods and techniques will probably continue to be rather inefficient but nonetheless moderately successful in the overwhelming majority of instances. Although most of the things that teachers currently do in classrooms are based on personal bias and tradition, those who claim that they could do dramatically better under the conditions in which teachers now work have yet to prove their case.

Because tradition plays such a large role in educational practice, and because schools severely limit procedures teachers can apply just by their organizational structure, rules, and facilities, the variation in instructional procedures found in schools is not very great when one seriously considers the range of possibilities. One may guess, then, that the kinds of abilities schools do develop are considerably more limited than is necessary.

* For a description of one computer device see L. F. Carter. Automated instruction. *Amer. Psychol.*, 1961, 16, 705–710.

The Effects of Schooling

Strictly speaking, in order to judge the consequences of formal education on an individual's personality and abilities it would be necessary to know what would have happened to him had he not gone to school. In a country where virtually everybody gets at least some formal education and where 60 per cent of the population will graduate from high school, investigation of this topic is hampered. Certainly there are not likely to be many studies that would keep some children out of school just for experimental purposes. Instead it is necessary to compare groups who differ in amount and kind of education for other reasons, which means that all

6

sorts of artifacts enter into the data. Those things that appear to be results of these differences in education may be the causes of them, or both the differences and their apparent consequences may be caused by something else. For example, it is common to urge students to finish high school because graduates earn more than dropouts. But it is possible that the factors that lead these individuals to graduate are also the factors that enable them to earn more money. One could argue that the brighter individuals tend to get more schooling because they are brighter and tend to earn more money, not because of more schooling but again because they are brighter. Then again, perhaps schooling makes one brighter; the circle can be run in any order. In short, almost all the information to be offered in this chapter is subject to various interpretations.

As one might guess from the material presented in the preceding chapters, quite a bit is known about how much knowledge students acquire in school, a bit less about the abilities they develop, still less about the development and change of attitudes, values, and beliefs, and relatively little about changes in basic motivational patterns that occur because of schooling. For the last of these categories it will suffice to say that changes in needs and drives of individuals as a result of their school experiences do seem to occur; what these changes are depends on such things as the degree of correspondence between the environmental press in school, home, and community, the individual's original personality patterns when he entered school, his abilities, and so on. It would be farfetched to claim that at present schools could realistically either plan to change personality patterns or adequately assess any changes for which they might be responsible.

On the other hand, changes in student knowledge are carefully planned and are readily, albeit imperfectly, measured. In this area mountains of data are available. The manuals for interpreting scores of hundreds of standardized achievement tests report information concerning the relationship between age and knowledge, grade and knowledge, intelligence and knowledge, and so forth. This information is pretty much what one would expect. People who have studied something know more about it than those who haven't. The higher the grade a student has completed the more likely he is to have a large body of general information; the relation of such knowledge to time spent in school is not as great. Age norms and grade norms indicate not only the average effects of amount of schooling but also the range and frequency of variations in these effects, and many of the factors identified with these variations are known. A number of these factors are discussed in Chapter 2. In fact, we have now gone a full circle and are discussing as consequences of schooling those student characteristics earlier treated as variable factors affecting learning. Of course not all the matters mentioned in Chapter 2 are affected by schooling. Race and region of the country are obvious examples; however, the effect of, say, region on achievement is presumably not direct but appears because of its relation to such things as effort. For example, those states that spend the most per pupil per year have substantially higher test score averages than those that spend the least.

Pupils in school today generally perform better than their counterparts of 40 and 50 years ago on most achievement tests, in spite of both the wider range of materials now presented and the larger proportion of children of a given age in school. Not that schooling leads to as much knowledge as is possible or ideal; still, most students acquire quite a lot of knowledge in school. Of course, the typical college professor often thinks the high schools do particularly badly in his own specialty just as many high school teachers tend to scorn the work of the elementary schools. Yardsticks for these comparisons are hard to come by, but if student interest and number of students who make regular progress in achievement are measures of quality, the elementary schools in this country are, on the average, better than both our high schools and colleges.

More debatable are the effects of schooling on attitudes and abilities. One reason is that gains in knowledge usually appear more quickly and are more easily measured than are changes in attitudes and abilities. Another possible reason is that all concerned—parents, teachers, pupils, the community at large —have a more explicit conception of the knowledge students are supposed to learn than they do of the abilities and attitudes to be developed. Educators are more likely to be working at cross purposes wittingly or unwittingly with respect to attitudes than they are with respect to knowledge.

EDUCATION AND ATTITUDE CHANGE

Attitudes are associated with many of the social and cultural factors affecting personality (social status, religion, regional customs, and so on). Amount and kind of education are also related to these same factors, so that the evidence frequently poses a "chicken and egg" problem of interpretation. In one of the few reports where the role of these factors could be accounted for, C. H. Stember attempted to assess the effect of level of education on various attitudes that would fall under the general heading of prejudice. He re-analyzed and summarized reports of over two dozen national surveys, such as the Gallup poll and the Roper poll, obtained during the 1940's and 1950's. Since these polls obtain expressed opinions, the phrasing of each question and the time at which it was asked are factors which affect the results obtained. Interestingly, it appears that both the least educated and the most educated are more variable over time, shift more as phrasing shifts, and are more likely to differ by social class and region than is the case among the intermediate groups. Stember's major conclusions were:

> In brief, the educated are *less likely* to:
> hold *traditional* stereotypes;
> favor discriminatory *policies;*
> reject *casual* contacts with minority-group members.
> The educated are *more likely* to:
> hold certain highly charged and derogatory stereotypes;
> favor *informal* discrimination in some areas of behavior;
> reject *intimate* contacts with minority-group members.

From Stember's data it appears that for the most part education affects the way in which prejudices and attitudes towards minority groups are expressed. Well-educated individuals are sensitive to "inappropriate" ways of expressing prejudice; and although the college graduate or college student is likely to support full legal equality, full social participation is another matter. The educated usually reject the vocabulary of the out-and-out bigot and express wishes for equality and justice; but for particular questions such as, "Would you have a Negro next-door neighbor?" level of education alters answers differently in different social groups, as Table 16 illustrates.

TABLE 16

Some Effects of Education and Social Class on Opinions of Whites about Association with Negroes (1944)

Level of Education	Social Class			All Classes
	Lower	Middle	Upper	
I. "Would it make any difference to you if a Negro family moved in next door to you?" (Percentage answering "No")				
Grammar school	27	24	37	26
Some high school	26	24	16	24
Completed high school	29	19	20	21
College	68	24	14	23
II. "Do you think you would eat at a restaurant that served both white and Negro people?" (Percentage answering "Yes")				
Grammar school	49	49	65	49
Some high school	52	50	64	52
Completed high school	60	50	55	54
College	83	65	59	63

Adapted from C. H. Stember. *Education and attitude change.* New York: Institute of Human Relations Press, 1961, pp. 128, 129, 133.

Only college experiences seemed to alter the more deeply rooted prejudices, and Stember asserts, "In a sense, this finding bears out our earlier conclusion, that the influence of education is more superficial than profound—reaching most strongly those aspects of prejudice which are least entrenched in the normative system." He nevertheless concludes that, to the degree any differences in prejudice are found among various groups in this country, amount of education is the most positive factor identifiable from these surveys.

Stember also reports data suggesting that the particular course of study taken by a college student may make a difference. Students in the social sciences tend to show a decrease in prejudicial attitudes during their college years, whereas students in other areas, business for example, do not. There is some indication that when college students have opportunities to associate with other racial and ethnic groups, the effects of education have a greater chance of functioning, and reductions in prejudice do occur.

The positive effects of college experience found by Stember are significant only by contrast with the changes attributable to high school experience. That most changes, including those at the college level, are in the direction of conformity is a widely accepted conclusion. It has been claimed that the large majority of college students in recent years find the world pretty much to their liking and encounter nothing in college that affects their values and beliefs. In summarizing data on this matter, H. Webster, M. Freedman, and P. Heist report that the studies on attitudes and values "carried out prior to the end of World War II showed that in general students in college changed in the direction of greater liberalism and sophistication in their political, social, and religious outlooks. There was also evidence of broadening interest during the college years." They also report that recent studies of particular attitudes and values have shown changes resembling those reported before 1945. One example of the kind of data on which they base this assertion is shown in Table 17, which indicates again that field of study is relevant but that a large majority of the students did not change their views regardless of course of study.

TABLE 17

Responses of National Merit Scholars to the Question:
"Should Government Provide Medical and Dental Care
for Citizens Who Cannot Afford Such Services?"

	End of Freshman Year		End of Junior Year	
	Yes	No	Yes	No
Group	(in percentages)		(in percentages)	
Engineering—men	56	29	47	42
Mathematics—men	55	19	70	11
Humanities—men	57	38	77	22
Humanities—women	50	39	61	26

From H. Webster, M. Freedman, and P. Heist. Personality changes in college students. In N. Sanford (ed.). *The American college.* New York: Wiley, 1962, p. 827.

It is possible to consider this lack of change as something to be "viewed with alarm," especially because of the apparently lesser shift in opinion to be found among high school students. H. H. Remmers and D. H. Radler, in summarizing the results of the Purdue Opinion Polls given over a 15-year period, infer from the data presented in Table 18 that "These opinions demonstrate that the American teenager does not believe wholeheartdly in the Bill of Rights but disagrees with six major provisions." Since presumably almost everyone would claim to support the Constitution, an indictment of American schools seems possible although a majority stand with the Constitution on half of these provisions. Also, it should be noted that although the changes are small, for five of these six statements the higher the level of education the more the agreement with the specific provision of the Bill of Rights. Furthermore, the authors note that the opinions of teenagers are substantially those of their parents, which are not markedly dissimilar from those of the teachers in the schools.

TABLE 18

Opinions about Statements Based on the Bill of Rights among American High School Students (1951)

Statement Presented to Students	Grade	Agree	Disagree	Uncertain
		(in percentages)		
Newspapers and magazines should be allowed to print anything they want except military secrets.	9	50	37	13
	10	43	41	16
	11	39	46	14
	12	46	43	11
The government should prohibit some people from making public speeches.	9	38	50	12
	10	31	54	15
	11	34	54	12
	12	32	57	11
In some cases, the police should be allowed to search a person or his home even though they do not have a warrant.	9	31	64	5
	10	26	68	6
	11	24	71	5
	12	20	76	4
Certain groups should not be allowed to hold public meetings even though they gather peaceably and only make speeches.	9	28	56	16
	10	22	62	16
	11	24	63	12
	12	24	64	12
Persons who refuse to testify against themselves (that is, give evidence that would show that they are guilty of criminal acts) should either be made to talk or severely punished.	9	37	41	22
	10	33	46	21
	11	30	51	19
	12	29	55	16
Some of the petitions which have been circulated should not be allowed by the government.	9	35	29	36
	10	35	30	35
	11	33	37	30
	12	32	43	25

Adapted from H. H. Remmers and D. H. Radler. *The American teenager.* Indianapolis: Bobbs-Merrill, 1957, pp. 210, 212, 216.

These facts permit the following conclusions:

1. Basic patterns of values and beliefs are not usually established by schools, nor are they readily changed by schools.

2. Schools may have some effect on specific attitudes related to a portion of the value and belief patterns of an individual.

3. Rather strong effects on the form in which attitudes are expressed are rather common. Since in most cases schools represent the values and beliefs of the community which they serve, they play a major role in teaching students accepted ways of expressing their beliefs and values.

4. The attitudes of a child are likely to be those of the people around him, although both knowledge and direct experience may play a role. The less

relevant knowledge and experience a student has the more important the opinions of the adults in his environment will be. In particular, the political, social, and religious values of young people are likely to be formed through contact with the attitudes of others, either directly or vicariously through reading, seeing a film, or the like.

From this it follows that schools can form and change attitudes fairly readily by direct instruction when they have the field to themselves, that is, when students do not encounter opposing opinions outside of school. This is an unlikely event when the the attitudes are about matters people generally consider important. And furthermore, a good deal of effort is expended by many citizens to see to it that the schools do not present opinions opposing their own. Remmers and Radler report that the effect of having taken a civics course was as often negative as positive. The research on attempts to teach attitudes that would prevent the development of an antagonism and prejudice between races indicates that positives effects appear only when teachers have genuine beliefs in agreement with their efforts, when they express these beliefs explicitly, and when they themselves are sensitive to the feelings of the children in their classrooms. It seems probable that civics courses do not have the effects one might anticipate because many constitutional questions are so "controversial" that some teachers do not believe changes in student attitude are needed and others prefer or are told to avoid discussions of these issues. Thus, the conditions for change of belief are often lacking. When teachers avoid emotional issues it is unlikely that they are going to have any effect on the attitudes of their students. It is, of course, also possible that under these circumstances schools have little effect of any sort on their students.

The reason why college experience seems to have a stronger influence on such attitudes than does high school education may be a function of two factors. First, college students are more likely to encounter other students who come from different backgrounds with different values; the values of a college faculty too are likely to be diverse and strongly expressed. Of course, encountering new points of view can be distressing and can produce shifts away from as easily as towards the new opinion. Secondly, direct experience, which is the other potent factor in attitude change, has a greater opportunity to function. Students in college have more opportunities to have really new experiences that may lead to attitude change than they are likely to have in their local high school.

In any case, regardless of the educational level in question, the particular attitudes most strongly influenced by education are not always those with which the institutions are overtly concerned. Statements of school policy often proclaim a desire to change students in ways that are neither accomplished nor seriously desired. Many communities would be appalled if all the graduates of their high schools developed strong scholarly values. By the same token, acceptance by students of the status quo is rarely a stated goal of school instruction but may nonetheless be deliberately and skillfully accomplished. This ambivalence on the part of schools toward the attitudes developed by their students does not at first glance seem to have a parallel in the area of ability development. However, to the degree that attitudes and abilities grow together in related patterns, schools may not be as eager to develop some abilities as they claim. The attitudes that accompany high creativity, such as the relatively low estimate of the values associated with adult success, could be a bit hard to take in large numbers of students. Considering the preference of teachers for the high IQ students found in the Getzels and Jackson study, it seems at least possible that the stated goal of many schools to "develop the potential abilities of their students" does not entirely represent either school practice or intention.

After using knowledge and ability as separate entities for so many pages it may be well to reiterate that achievement tests and other measures of knowledge can be considered tests of ability heavily weighted with the cognitive abilities. Schooling clearly affects the cognitive abilities in a strong, systematic fashion, but since the use of separate tests of the various abilities has not been widespread, it is necessary to rely on data from general intelligence tests to judge what schooling contributes to ability over and above its effect on knowledge. Intelligence tests generally sample a greater range of abilities than do achievement tests, and if formal education has a lasting effect on intelligence test scores it is fair to conclude that more than knowledge has been changed. There is such evidence.

First, there are the facts that (a) mental age (MA) tends to level off at about the age when most people leave school—at or near the end of high school, (b) continued increases in MA beyond the age range 16–19 are more common among those continuing in school than among those leaving school, and (c) a decline in MA is less noticeable among those adults in occupations that require much activity similar to school study, such as teaching, medicine, law, and the like. These points may be, but need not be, considered evidence that schooling has a powerful influence on intelligence.

Second, there is the frequently obtained result that highest grade reached is correlated with IQ. A. Anastasi, who has summarized much of the data on this topic, says (1958, pp. 205–206):

The effect of schooling upon intellectual development has also been explored through an analysis of the relationship between amount of education and intelligence test scores on adults. For example, surveys conducted in the American army during both world wars yielded correlations of .73 and .74 between intelligence tests (Army Alpha or AGCT) and highest grade reached in school. There are, of course, two alternative explanations for such correlations: (1) education raises the intellectual level, and (2) the brighter individuals are more likely to "survive" the increasingly stringent selection of successive educational levels. That the duration of any one individual's education is not entirely dependent upon his ability is fairly obvious. Financial resources, family tradition and attitudes, educational facilities in different localities, and a number of other nonintellectual factors can readily be cited. On the other hand, considerable intellectual selection undoubtedly does occur at successive educational levels beyond the compulsory grades.

Lorge has reported data that lend support to both of Anastasi's alternatives. He retested 131 men who had been given intelligence tests 20 years earlier while in the eighth grade. His results, shown in Table 19, indicate that both initial score and amount of subsequent education are related to the later scores. Those scoring high initially tend to score high later; but at all levels of initial score, those with the most schooling tend to have gained in relative standing. The correlation between final standing and highest grade reached was .67, whereas that between highest grade reached and initial standing was only .36. The partial correlation—that is, a correlation with the effect of a third variable, here initial score, held constant—between final score and grade level was .61, a figure which differs little from that between initial and final score (.64, or .58 partial). Thus, further schooling had just as much to do with adult ability as did ability in the eighth grade.

TABLE 19

Mean Intelligence Test Scores of 131 Men Arranged by Initial Score in the Eighth Grade 20 Years Earlier and by Highest Grade Completed Thereafter

Highest Grade Completed	Initial Score Category		
	Low	Average	High
15 or more	34	40	52
11–14	23	31	40
8–10	20	26	38

Adapted from Irving Lorge. Schooling makes a difference. *Teach. Coll. Rec.*, 1945, 46, 483–492.

Other studies have obtained similar results, and a reasonable interpretation of these data is that schooling does indeed raise intelligence and that lack of schooling may lower it. But to reiterate, "Obviously, a conclusive answer can be obtained only with the type of experimental design in which the experimenter decides who shall and who shall not continue his education at each level and assigns the subjects at random to the different educational groups." * Still imperfect, but more nearly to the point, are reports from recent attempts to alter the pattern of achievement among "culturally deprived" children. This pattern was described earlier (see pp. 25–27), and it was noted then that these children may show a decline in intelligence as they get older even though they remain, more or less, "in school."

The preliminary reports of two major efforts undertaken recently in New York City and St. Louis are available. In New York the Demonstration Guidance Project was directed at the early identification and stimulation of able students (the top 50 per cent) drawn from culturally deprived homes and backgrounds in an effort to compensate for this deprivation. The program included enrichment of the child's cultural life, the enrichment and adaptation of the curriculum to the pupil's needs, an effort to supply remedial services especially in reading, and an effort to educate the parents about the

* *Ibid.*, p. 208.

importance of the school in helping their children develop their abilities. An increased guidance staff worked with teachers, parents, and administrators as well as with pupils. Volunteers, parents, and teachers were used to help score tests, to help on field trips, and to man before- and after-school study sessions. Community agencies and successful people from disadvantaged backgrounds were called upon as resources, and theaters, museums, factories, and employment agencies were visited. The students spent extra time on remedial work and homework and used both school and outside time to attend cultural events, lectures, and field trips.

The initial group in the demonstration project was selected from seventh graders in a junior high school in 1956. Among the results for this group were the following: (1) 43 per cent of the graduates attended postsecondary schools, whereas in the past only 11 per cent went beyond high school; (2) the holding power of the school for the group was 64 per cent as compared with 47 per cent in prior years, and there was no attrition because of race; (3) the mean IQ for a sample of 81 members of the group changed from 93 in 1956 to 102 in 1959. For this group of 81 students the median individual gain was 13 IQ points in a three-year-three-month period. Sixty-six of the 81 scores increased, 12 dropped, and three remained the same. The proportion of scores over 140 changed from 2 to 12 per cent. Gain in reading scores was greater than for any comparable preproject group.

One of the central features of the program was the extensive effort made to involve parents. The project directors felt that in the kind of homes from which these children come the family too often works against the school— the parents do not give school work any importance, they do not help a child study (in fact the home is generally so crowded and noisy he cannot study), they know little about the school and do not trust it. Furthermore, such parents do not know how to help their children even when they want to help, so the program counselors tried to have at least one interview wtih each parent, and workshops for parents were held at the school. The project was explained, parents learned how they could help their children to do better in school, plans were made for reading sessions for parents and for trips for the children, and parents were encouraged to help form Boy Scout troops and instigate other activities. A monthly newsletter was sent out to keep parents posted on activities of the project and to give them hints about what they could do to enrich their child's life. For example, they were told which theaters were giving free tickets away, how to get to a zoo, or when a lecture was free and open to the public. In many cases this interest on the part of the school was a revelation to the parents, who had never had any positive relationship with schools before. This program has been expanded to include many schools and to start at grade three with no limitations on ability. The expanded program called the Higher Horizons Program has yielded improvements in achievement, attendance rates, discipline problems, and teacher morale.*

A similar sort of program is going on in St. Louis, Missouri, in the Banneker district, a lower-class and slum area. But in the Banneker project the emphasis is on motivation of pupils rather than on cultural enrichment and compensa-

* Statement of D. Schreiber to the Conference before the United States Commission on Civil Rights, February, 1961, Williamsburg, Va.

tion for deprivation. The first step taken in this program was to acquaint the principals, teachers, and parents with the harsh reality of where the students stood, not only in comparison to others in the area but also where they stood in comparison to national norms. Students were taught about the importance of school, of tests, and of achievement for success in high school and for getting jobs thereafter. Parents were similarly indoctrinated and asked to promise to oversee homework and told how to do it. Competition among students, classes, and schools was initiated. Field trips to show employment opportunities and standards were introduced to reinforce the desire for higher achievement. Summer school work was added. The emphasis throughout was on an effort to increase strength of drive and desire for success.

The results of the program are similar to those reported by Higher Horizons. Although the stated purposes of the two programs are different, with one emphasizing cultural enrichment and the other increased aspiration, in many respects their actual activities are also similar. The most notable common features are (1) the involvement of parents in the school work of their children, (2) the effort to bring students into greater contact with the larger community in which they live, (3) the positive attention aimed at giving each student the impression that perhaps he is somebody who counts, (4) the emphasis on reading, study skills, and supervised study. It seems reasonable to assume that the consequences of these programs have been changes in both abilities and attitudes and that one change could not have occurred without the other. Again it appears that abilities and motivational traits are inseparable.*

Schools can produce positive changes in students' IQ's as well as in their attitudes towards school and towards life. Yet the typical Negro schools in the South and slum schools across the nation produce or permit negative changes, while the large majority of the schools in the country leave average IQ's unchanged. However, individual IQ's of children change frequently; some increase steadily, others decline, many fluctuate. Most children change five or more points between any two testings spread over a year or more; many change by 20 or 25 points. Nevertheless, the mean IQ for most groups of children in most schools is a quite stable figure, changing only two or three points over periods of several years. This last fact calls for explanation.

Generally speaking, the kind and quality of schooling a child receives can be predicted from the kind and quality of home from which he comes. Under normal circumstances, therefore, changes in IQ for groups of students in a given school are not to be expected. This does not mean that the schools do not contribute to the abilities of the students. It means they make the expected contribution to the abilities of students, the amount one would predict on the basis of other sorts of information. Perhaps changes in ability occur only when the school deviates from what one would expect.

It seems reasonable to assume that (a) when a school's program is closed off from the rest of a student's life, the school is making less of a contribution to his ability than one might anticipate, (b) when schools are reasonably

* For a brief description of this program and many others, see J. St. Clair Price. *Improving the academic performances of Negro students.* Research Committee of the Association of Colleges and Secondary Schools, 1959.

coordinated with the child's background they make about the expected contribution, and (c) when they go into the child's life and in some way lead to serious changes in his circumstances, they may in fact raise his relative abilities as represented by the IQ. In the last instance, changes in cognitive style, and thus in values and beliefs, would probably ensue.

EPILOGUE

The psychological principles illustrated by reports of programs like Banneker and Higher Horizons have great generality quite aside from the importance of the social problems of deprived groups. As a case in point, we may conclude this book by considering the relationships between psychology and education. By now it should be clear that psychological problems pervade those of education. Yet psychologists and educators alike have made little use of the knowledge available in each other's domain. In practice the efforts of educators to use psychological knowledge have been superficial. The fads and fancies of educators with respect to grouping practices is just one example. Similarly, academic psychologists have typically ignored information about educational methods—witness the tradition-bound instructional procedures of most psychology departments. Although there have been hopeful signs of change during the last few years in both groups, it is evident that only changes in their attitudes and values, or their learning sets and abilities, can really improve matters. The sheer acquisition of knowledge will not accomplish this.

Education students at all levels would do well to study educational psychology as a way of thinking about educational problems, as a way of finding out about some of the dimensions of learning situations, and as a way of doing research relevant to educational problems. But the traditional approach has been to study educational psychology as a body of knowledge which can dictate teaching procedures, and this approach is probably a waste of time. The amount and kind of knowledge available in educational psychology is such that its ready transfer to school situations is exceedingly difficult and is unlikely to be successful unless new ways of thinking are developed. Students can of course be told how a principle applies to a particular school situation. But it has long been evident that the set created by this kind of instruction is not helpful to teachers. In spite of periodic statements to the effect that the millenium is here, psychological knowledge remains too scanty for its application to the complexities of classroom situations to be anything but an art. The small advances that have been made do not alter the fact that direct studies of school learning continue to be badly, if not desperately, needed.

In an analogous fashion, students of psychology could profitably consider schools as proper settings for research, examine the relevance of some of the research on educational questions for psychological theory, and personally face the gap between the psychological principles they are studying and their own educational practices or those of their instructors. The tradition of denying interest in the "practical" problems of education, or of ignoring them as too complex to be dealt with, has often led to unnecessarily narrow views of psychological problems. For example, a consideration of schooling and intelligence raises questions about the relation between the development of intelligence and transfer, but this topic has received relatively little attention since Thorndike studied the matter many years ago.

It may appear that the preceding statements are merely saying that both educators and psychologists should become educational psychologists. Since both have unique and legitimate problems of little interest to the other, this view is clearly absurd. But it is almost as absurd to ask educational psychologists to bridge the gap unaided. Having to do so in the face of the very different attitudes and kinds of abilities of psychologists and educators has meant that educational psychologists have had the choice of working in a limbo unable to talk to either group, developing a cognitive style in tune with just one of the two groups while ignoring the other, or, in a rather schizoid fashion, trying to jump back and forth between the two.

It seems reasonable to suggest that progress in education, in psychology, and hence in educational psychology, would be enhanced by the development of more educators who find it natural to treat some of their problems from the point of view of an experimental psychologist, and by the development of more psychologists who reverse this approach. But it should be emphasized that this is not a call for complete personality transformations, since sharp changes can lead to unexpected results. The following tale which appeared recently in *Sports Illustrated* indicates what can happen when really dramatic changes in personality occur, whether one calls them changes in cognitive style, in values and beliefs, or in abilities and learning sets:

There was a time when a little lamb could be counted on to act like one, to be gentle and meek and to follow Mary, but in Watford in Hertfordshire, there is a sheep which chases around with sheep dogs, eats dog food, walks on a lead, answers to his name, senses like a dog, smells like a dog, and refuses to take any stuff off a dog because, poor dreamer, he thinks he is one. The schizophrenic is named Larry and he was raised with puppies in a National Canine Defense League program to help cure bad dogs of sheep worrying (savage pestering). To pull wool over Larry's eyes, trainer Frank Petit starved him for 24 hours, then put him in a compound with a sheep-chasing sheep dog and a bowl of food. Larry doggedly held his own, even with tough Alsatians. Said Petit: "He sent them flying with a butt of his head. They limped away, shocked." . . . Police are now sending sheep worriers to Petit instead of having them destroyed. Dale Carnegie should do so well. Petit has had eighteen successful personality transformations without a miss. Larry, good sheep dog that he is, has in the meanwhile become Petit's special pet. The only snag in his metamorphosis was the day Petit put him into a field with some other sheep. He chased them.*

* From, Living like a dog. *Sports Illustrated,* June 24, 1963, pp. 6, 8. Reprinted from *Scorecard* by special permission of *Sports Illustrated,* Time, Inc.

Selected Readings

The books on this list provide more extensive discussions and in some cases alternate views of one or more of the topics in this book. A few of the books cover all of the topics; for the rest, the boldface numbers indicate the chapters in the book most closely related to the material in the reference.

Anastasi, A. *Differential psychology*. 3rd ed. New York: Macmillan, 1958. **2, 6**

Bruner, J. S. *The process of education*. Cambridge: Harvard University Press, 1960. **3, 4, 5**

Bugelski, B. R. *The psychology of learning*. New York: Holt, Rinehart and Winston, 1960. **4, 5**

Charters, W. W. and N. L. Gage. *Readings in the social psychology of education*. Boston: Allyn and Bacon, 1963.

Coleman, J. S. *The adolescent society*. New York: Macmillan, 1961. **3, 4**

Cronbach, L. J. *Educational psychology*. 2nd ed. New York: Harcourt, Brace, and World, 1963.

Festinger, L. *A theory of cognitive dissonance*. New York: Harper & Row, 1957. **4**

Gage, N. L. (Ed.) *Handbook of research on teaching*. Chicago: Rand McNally, 1963. **5**

Havighurst, R. J., P. H. Bowman, C. V. Matthews, and J. V. Pierce. *Growing up in River City*. New York: Wiley, 1962. **2**

Henry, N. B. (Ed.) *Individualizing instruction*. 61st Yearbook of the National Society for the Study of Education, Part I. Chicago: University of Chicago Press, 1962. **2, 3**

Hunt, J. McV. *Intelligence and experience*. New York: Ronald, 1961. **2, 4, 6**

James, W. *Principles of psychology*. New York: Holt, 1890.

Judd, C. H. *Education as cultivation of the higher mental processes*. New York: Macmillan, 1936. **3, 4**

Klausmeier, H. J. *Learning and human abilities: educational psychology*. New York: Harper & Row, 1960.

Lazarus, R. S. *Personality and adjustment*. Englewood Cliffs, New Jersey: Prentice-Hall, 1963. **2, 6**

McClelland, D. C., J. W. Atkinson, R. A. Clark, and E. L. Lowell. *The achievement motive*. New York: Appleton-Century-Crofts, 1953. **2, 4**

McDonald, F. J. *Educational psychology*. San Francisco: Wadsworth, 1959.

McGeoch, J. A. and A. L. Irion. *The psychology of human learning*. 2nd ed. New York: Longmans, Green, 1952. **3, 4**

Mednick, S. *Learning*. Englewood Cliffs, New Jersey: Prentice-Hall, 1964. **4**

Reissman, F. *The culturally deprived child*. New York: Harper & Row, 1962. **2, 6**

Sarason, S. B., K. S. Davidson, F. F. Lighthall, R. R. Waite, and B. K. Ruebush. *Anxiety in elementary school children*. New York: Wiley, 1960. **2, 4**

Terman, L. M. and M. Oden. *The gifted child grows up*. Stanford, California: Stanford University Press, 1947. **2**

Thorndike, E. L. *Educational psychology, Volume I: The original nature of man. Volume II: The psychology of learning*. New York: Teachers College, Columbia University, 1913.

Trow, W. C. *Teacher and technology*. New York: Appleton-Century-Crofts, 1963. **5**

Index

A